BY THE
MYSTERY CHEFS

BOXTREE

First published in Great Britain in
1992 by Boxtree Limited.

Text © Last-Ditch
Television 1992.
Illustrations
© Andy Barber 1992.

10 9 8 7 6 5 4 3 2 1

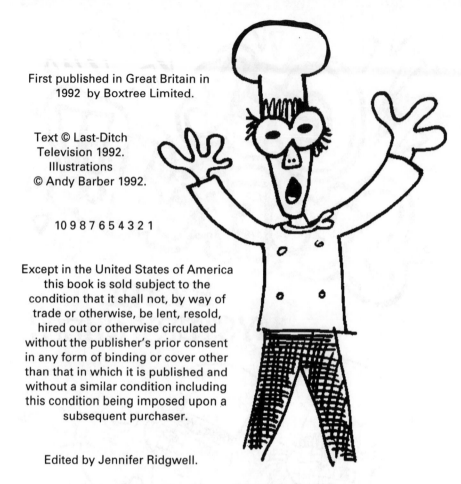

Edited by Jennifer Ridgwell.

Designed and typeset by Anita Ruddell.
Printed and bound in Great Britain by Redwood Press for

Boxtree Limited
Broadwall House
21 Broadwall
London SE1 9PL

A CIP catalogue entry for this book is available from the British Library.

ISBN 1 85283 404 8

CONTENTS:

A BIT OF DRIVEL:

Once upon a time normal people used to marvel at the culinary antics of a gang of television-star chefs, who swaggered around studio kitchens showing off and pretending to teach you how to cook stuff you'd probably never even heard of. Then, the telly got groovy and **GET STUFFED!!** arrived with a crazy, ambitious mission to make normal people show us what they really cook for themselves at home. So, we give our thanks to the hundreds of poor, unwitting souls who have appeared in the series and we hope that this book will give you the information and courage to 'get down' in your kitchen and cook some of the stuff that you've seen on **GET STUFFED!!**

But before we get going, you're probably anxious to know where the wild, freaky **GET STUFFED!!** inspiration comes from... aren't you? Well, here's a clue, and a bit of a long-winded background to boot!

Have you ever crashed one of those parties where some poor goon's house has been invaded by an army of drunken strangers, and every room has had a few cushions scattered on the floor and been given a 'Purpose'? There's the 'Loud Music Room', with the domestic hi-fi coughing its guts out, pretending it's at Wembley; the 'Smart Alec Room', where bores boast about their preoccupations, be they anything from mortgages to motor-bikes; the 'Sex Room', usually with a burning joss-stick, where you had hoped you'd meet the babe of your dreams but which has been commandeered by couples already in love who want to flaunt it. So, in desperation, you hit the kitchen and – hey, man – it's really neat in there, and there's all this fantastic stuff you can play with! Flour! Water! Salt! Chocolate! And the kitchen's full of all the other party misfits!! So you start grooving around and before you know it – wow, everyone's having a great time and you've just invented Chocolate Chapatis! And if you're poor enough, mad enough and weird enough, and do this sort of thing often enough – you'll probably end up as a fairly plausible cook, or even a Mystery Chef!

And that's where **GET STUFFED!!** is coming from because, believe it or not, the Mystery Chefs really do make and create **GET STUFFED!!**, and us Chefs know what we're talking about. Firstly, we're pleasure-loving beasts who have been broke, desperate and hungry, yet we still want to eat like kings, albeit on a shoestring. Secondly, we get a weird kick from charging into other people's kitchens – from the best to the worst – grabbing cooks by the throat, making them prepare excellent meals for us, then demanding their recipes. Yes sir – you'll find it all in this book, from Michelin star cuisine, to ferreting off the pavement for scraps at the end of a busy market.

And inside our kitchen, it's hotter, louder and groovier than any night-club you can afford to visit. So follow our lead – take time to perfect your skill and don't worry about experimenting with different quantities or new ingredients. Most importantly, don't be afraid to go WILD in your kitchen!

SO, WHO ARE THESE WONDERFULLY TALENTED, HANDSOME AND ERUDITE MYSTERY CHEFS? WELL, THAT WOULD BE TELLING WOULDN'T IT?

LUNCH SNACKS:

If you wanna do away with convention,
Try some of our lunchtime inventions.

EGGY TOASTIES

Who needs a toasted-sandwich maker? Chuck it out and use your frying-pan instead. Here's how to make your very own eggy-weggy, deluxe sarnies...

Shopping:

1 egg
Salt and pepper
1 onion
Oil

4 slices bread
Tomatoes
Cheese

Beat the egg with a fork, add salt and pepper. Chop half the onion and add to the egg. Heat the oil in a frying-pan. Dunk 2 slices of bread in the eggy mixture until it is completely basted and then place in the frying-pan. Turn the bread over when browned. Slice the cheese and tomatoes, and chop up the rest of the onion. Place the cheese and tomato on 1 piece of bread and the cheese and onion on the other. When the cheese has melted, sandwich together the sides with the fillings and you have your own special home-brand of toasted sarnie.

CHAPATIS

Chapatis are an Indian-style bread and you can buy special chapati pans to make them in, or you can just use an ordinary frying-pan. Kneading that dough will give you strong fingers to massage all your friends!

Shopping:

8 oz plain flour
Pinch of salt
Water

Lettuce
Cheese

Put the flour and salt into a bowl and mix in a little water until you have enough to form a dough. Knead the mixture then divide the dough into small balls, about the size of golf balls. Roll the balls out on a floured surface with a rolling pin or milk bottle until they are quite thin. Place the chapatis in a hot frying-pan – do not use any oil – and fry on each side for about 1 minute until they are just starting to turn brown and form bubbles. Take each chapati out of the pan and hold with a spatula over the gas flame or electric ring, making sure they do not touch the heat source and burn – this is enough to finish off the cooking and make them crisper. Grate some cheese, shred some lettuce and roll it up in the chapati, or just serve them with an Indian meal.

Mystery Chef announcement:

'You don't need plates so there is no washing up – brilliant!'

CROSTINI

Crostini actually means 'small crusts'. It's a sort of poor man's pizza – or a very rich man's Welsh Rarebit! It's excellent as a hearty snack..

Shopping:

4 slices white bread
Milk
Oil
Ham slices
Mozzarella/Cheddar

1 tin tomatoes, chopped
Basil
Parsley
Salt

Slice the bread and brush one side with milk. Grease a baking tray with oil and lay in it the bread, milky side up. Put a slice of ham on each piece of bread, followed by slices of Mozzarella or Cheddar. Open the tomatoes and spoon some on the cheese. Sprinkle on the basil, parsley and salt – the tomato juice will soak up the herbs. Cook under the grill for about 5 minutes, or in the oven for 10 minutes on 180°C (350°F, Gas Mark 4).

9

ENGLISH RAREBIT

This is an adaptable sort of recipe which can be Welsh Rarebit disguised as English Rarebit, or it can even be a fondue if you put too much beer in it. You can also try putting anchovies on the toast before you pour on the cheesy goo.

Shopping:

4 slices bread
Masses of cheese
Butter
$\frac{1}{2}$ can beer
1 tablespoon cornflour
Mustard
Worcester sauce
Salt and pepper
Parsley
Anchovies (optional)

Toast and butter the bread. Grate the cheese. Melt the butter in a pan and add half the beer and all the cheese. Heat it gently until all the cheese has melted. Blend the cornflour and a little of the remaining beer and pour into the pan - keep stirring as it thickens otherwise it will go lumpy. Add the mustard, Worcester sauce and seasoning. Arrange the toast in a shallow ovenproof dish and pour the cheese mixture over the top. Place the sloppy mess under a pre-heated grill until it's bubbly and golden. Garnish with parsley.

SPICED MINCE WITH PITTA BREAD

An easy spicy mince recipe which would be just as good on rice or couscous as in pitta bread. The green peas and red pepper give this attractive colours.

Shopping:

Oil
¾ lb minced beef
1 red pepper
Black pepper
Thyme
Paprika

Chilli powder
1 packet frozen peas
Tomato purée
Pitta bread
Lettuce, tomato and
  cucumber

Heat the oil in a frying-pan and add the mince to brown. De-core and chop the red pepper, add to the pan. Add the black pepper, thyme, paprika and chilli powder to make it really hot. A few frozen peas give the mixture more colour, together with a squirt of tomato purée. Toast the pitta bread lightly and slice it open. Fill the pitta bread with the mince and salad.

11

HUMMUS

A party dip favourite... that you can make at home by the bucket-load.

Shopping:

1 tin chick peas
Garlic
2 lemons
2 tablespoons tahini

Olive oil
Salt and pepper
Pitta bread

Drain the tin of chick peas and mash them up. Add the crushed garlic and lemon juice to the chick peas and mix it all in. Add the tahini, a little dash of olive oil, the seasoning and mash all the ingredients together. Serve with hot or cold pitta bread.

STUFFED PEPPERS

This has the same sort of sauce that you use for Spaghetti Ragu and numerous other Italian dishes. You can buy really grotty peppers for this; you won't be able to tell when they're cooked and they're so much cheaper.

Shopping:

1 onion
Oil
½ lb minced beef
Salt and pepper
1 tin tomatoes

1 red pepper
1 green pepper
Butter/margarine
Cheese

Chop the onion and fry in the oil. Add the mince to the pan with salt and pepper, keep stirring as the meat browns. Add the tomatoes and simmer for 5 minutes or so. Cut the peppers in half lengthwise and de-seed. Lay the peppers in a greased ovenproof dish and fill with the sauce. Put in the oven for 50 minutes at 180°C (350°F, Gas Mark 4). Take the peppers out of the oven and cover in grated cheese. Then put back into the oven for about 5–10 minutes for the cheese to melt.

STUFFED MUSHROOMS

Information bulletin for 'fungacines' everywhere: I bet you didn't know that mushrooms had hats and little feet – so cute, but for this recipe the feet have to be amputated!

Shopping:

8 big mushrooms
Lemon juice
1 onion
3 cloves garlic
Parsley
2–3 slices ham

Oil
Salt and pepper
1 vegetable stock cube
Butter/margarine
Breadcrumbs

Rinse the mushrooms and separate the feet from the hats. Chop the feet into little pieces and squeeze lemon juice over them. Chop the onion, garlic, parsley and ham, then fry them all in oil and season. Add boiling water to the stock cube and stir. Place the mushroom hats in a greased oven dish and fill them with the mixture from the frying-pan. Pour over the stock and sprinkle with breadcrumbs. Put into the oven for 20 minutes at 200°C (400°F, Gas Mark 6) –

et c'est parfait.

KARTOFFEL PUFFER

The German work ethic knows no bounds when it comes to doing complicated things with potatoes.

Shopping:
4 whopping potatoes
1 onion
2–3 eggs

2 tablespoons flour
Oil
Apple sauce

Peel and grate the potatoes. Grate the onion, add to the potatoes and then leave to stand in a bowl for a little while for the liquid and solid to separate. Spoon off as much of the liquid as possible. If you have a snazzy thing like a liquidizer, you can dispense with the grater! Crack and whisk the eggs and add to the potato slop. Sprinkle in enough flour to thicken the mixture. Then fry dollops of the stuff in hot oil and turn when they begin to brown. Serve your 'potato disguised as a pancake' with oodles of apple sauce. This is a popular lunchtime snack in Germany.

KARTOFFELKLOSS MIT SPECKSOSS

Alias a German potato dumpling with sausage in a bacon sauce – but you knew that already, didn't you? Very tasty, if a little complicated.

Shopping:

$\frac{1}{2}$ leek
Butter
2 smoked sausages, cooked
2 lb potatoes, raw
2 lb potatoes, cooked
2 eggs
Marjoram
Salt and pepper
Nutmeg
Flour
Stale bread

Sauce:
1 onion
6 rashers bacon, de-rinded
Oil
Butter
1 pint milk
Salt
Cornflour

Wash and slice the leek and fry in butter until it softens. Slice the sausage. Peel the raw potatoes and grate them with a cheese grater. Get out the juice by wringing the potato in a clean tea-towel. Mash the raw potato with the cooked potato and then bind together with the eggs. Add the cooked leeks, marjoram, salt, pepper, nutmeg and a sprinkling of flour. Cut a couple of slices of stale bread into cubes and mix in with the potatoes. Form the mixture into large balls, the size of your fist, and push a few pieces of sausage inside the middle of each ball. Carefully plunge the potato balls into a pan of boiling water, cover partially with a lid and simmer for 20 minutes.

For the sauce, slice the onion into rings and chop the bacon. Fry in hot oil and butter. When the onion begins to soften, add the milk, a pinch of salt and blend in the cornflour. Drain the potato balls and cover with the sauce.

LEEK AND POTATO SOUP

*This is a good, chunky soup –
excellent for a cold winter's day.*

Shopping:

2–3 potatoes
2 leeks
1 onion
2 carrots
2 celery sticks
Garlic
Butter

Oil
Salt and pepper
Paprika
Rosemary
1 vegetable stock cube
1 pint milk

Peel and cut the potatoes and parboil for 10 minutes. Top and tail the leeks and chop them roughly. Chop the onions, carrots, celery and garlic. Fry the paprika, salt, pepper, rosemary (pinch it from your neighbour's garden) – with the garlic in butter and oil. Add the onions, carrots, celery and potatoes to the pan, then add the prepared stock and milk. Simmer for 5 minutes, add the leeks and simmer for a further 10–15 minutes.

RUBBER GLOVES

NETTLE SOUP

This is so dangerous that you must wear protective clothing, so get out those bio-degradable rubber gloves (pink or yellow will do) for picking the nettles. Washing the nettles is also quite important, unless you like the taste of bird droppings. Nettles lose their sting as they cook, but if you are a paranoid sort of person, get some dock leaves ready in case. This meal will improve your psychic aura, man!

Shopping:

$\frac{1}{2}$ lb nettle leaves (tender
   top leaves are best)
1 onion
Garlic

Butter/margarine
Salt and pepper
3 pints boiling water
Soya milk/cream

If you can't find any nettles in the supermarket, try a ditch. Remove the leaves from the stalks and wash the leaves. Chop the onion and garlic and fry in melted butter/margarine. When the onion is soft add the nettles, salt, pepper and the boiling water. Mix it all in and boil for 5 minutes. Pour the soup into a liquidizer and then add a touch of soya milk to make it thicker.

EGGS:

When you crack an egg, don't eat the shell,
It'll stick in your throat and taste like Hell.

BACON AND EGG BAKE

A real crispy post-inebriation brunch, but very flavoursome and a different way of cooking eggs.

Shopping:

1 lb old potatoes	10 rashers bacon
1 onion	4 eggs
Oil	Black pepper

Peel the potatoes and dice into small chunks so they will cook more quickly. Peel and chop the onion and fry with the potato in hot oil for about 5 minutes with the lid on. Meanwhile, de-rind the bacon and cut up into thin strips. Add the bacon to the pan and fry until crispy – the fat from the bacon runs out into the other vegetables and gives them more flavour. Turn the mixture into an ovenproof dish and make 4 indents, breaking an egg into each one. Grind some pepper on top and cook in a pre-heated oven for 30 minutes at 180°C (350°F, Gas Mark 4).

Yum!

PERSIAN SCRAMBLED EGGS

A highly delicious but complicated way to make scrambled eggs which will test the technique of professional chefs. Remember not to pick your nose after chopping red chilli as it could be very painful, not to mention unhygienic!

Shopping:

1–2 shallots	3 eggs
Garlic	Oil
1 red chilli	Cumin
Coriander	Butter
Ginger	Cream
2 tomatoes	Salt and pepper

Chop up your shallots, garlic, chilli and coriander. Peel and grate the ginger. Peel and de-seed the tomatoes and chop finely. Whisk the eggs. Fry the shallots and garlic in hot oil, then add the ginger, chilli, cumin and a knob of butter. Add the eggs and scramble – with a whisk. When the eggs start to coagulate (what?) add the tomato, the coriander, a touch of cream, salt and pepper. Serve with sprinkled coriander on top.

MINUTES LATER... IT'S COOKED!

MUSHROOM OMELETTE

There is an art to cooking a good omelette to make it ultra-fluffy and lovely. You should use free range eggs because happy hens that run around and eat corn lay tastier eggs than birds who eat a lot of nasty stuff.

Shopping:

2–3 eggs   Few mushrooms
Salt and pepper   Butter
1 tablespoon water   Oil

Break the eggs into the bowl, add salt and pepper, then whisk. Also add the water, as during cooking this turns to steam and makes the omelette fluffier. Chop the mushrooms and fry in a knob of butter. Pour a little oil into another hot frying-pan – use oil because butter will burn. Pour the egg into the pan and whisk it round like scrambled egg until it is virtually set. At this point, leave it for a few seconds to set properly, put the mushrooms on top and fold the omelette over into a half-moon shape. Rub a little butter on to the omelette as a glaze and you have a really professional job.

EGG AND SALAMI SURPRISE

What's the surprise? Well, apart from the fact that your lower intestines will get a nasty one if you don't take the plastic rind off the sliced salami – surprise, surprise, it's an omelette.

Shopping:

Mushrooms
1 onion
Oil
Salami

6 eggs
4 oz cheese
Parsley

Slice the mushrooms and the onion (so you have aesthetically pleasing onion rings) and fry in oil in a preheated pan. Slice the salami, taking off the rind and add to the pan. Break the eggs into a bowl, whisk and then blend in the grated cheese and chopped parsley. Pour the egg over the cooked vegetables, leave for a few minutes and place under a pre-heated grill – making sure you don't melt the handle on the frying-pan!

EGG AND LENTIL BAKE

If you are a student you can eat a lot of lentils because they are very filling, very trendy and you can afford to feed all your friends, who will then scream and shout and be terribly happy that they are eating lentils with you.

Shopping:

1 packet red lentils	Oil
1 onion	1 tin tomatoes
Garlic	Sherry
1 green pepper	Parsley
1 red pepper	4 eggs

Put a couple of handfuls of lentils into boiling water and simmer for 20 minutes. Roughly chop up the onion, garlic and peppers, leaving half a green pepper to slice as a garnish. Fry the vegetables in oil and when they are soft, add the tomatoes. Strain the lentils and add them to the frying-pan with a dash of sherry, if you are wealthy enough to afford it, and add a sprinkling of chopped parsley. Stir, then leave to reduce down. After about 10 minutes pour into an ovenproof dish and make 4 small hollows in the mixture, breaking an egg into each one. Put the strips of green pepper in between the eggs and slam in the oven for 20 minutes at 180°C (350°F, Gas Mark 4).

BASIC QUICHE

This is the basic groundwork to any quiche and you can easily jazz it up by adding onion, cooked bacon, leeks, walnuts and other scrumptious stuff. You can also eat it hot or cold.

Mystery Chef social comment:
'The nouveau riche call it quiche, but the real man calls it flan!!'

Shopping:

8 large tablespoons flour	6 eggs
3 oz butter	Salt and pepper
Milk	Mixed herbs

Mix the flour and butter until it is the consistency of broken biscuits. Make a well in the mixture, pour in a little milk and carry on mixing until it binds. You can buy frozen pastry, but it won't taste as good as the home-made variety. Sprinkle flour on the work surface and roll out your pastry. Grease a tin and line with the pastry – covering the pastry with the greaseproof paper, then shove in the oven for 10 minutes at 180°C (350°F, Gas Mark 4). Break the eggs and whisk them with a little milk, salt, pepper and the herbs. Pour into the flan case and add any other stuff you fancy. Put the flan back into the oven for 20 minutes – 'eggcellent'.

24

CHEESY PIE

This may look like a school dinner, but it's not a school dinner and it certainly tastes better, honest! This is super cheesy, very good and unusual.

Shopping:

3 eggs
Salt and pepper
Cheese
1 teaspoon mustard

Bread
$\frac{1}{2}$ pint milk
Tomatoes

Break the eggs into a bowl, beat with a fork, then add salt and pepper. Grate a good handful of cheese and add it and the mustard to the eggs. Make some breadcrumbs using a liquidizer or a cheese grater. Meanwhile boil the milk. Mix the milk into the eggy stuff and then add the breadcrumbs to thicken the mixture. Pour into an ovenproof dish, slice some tomatoes and carefully place on top, the mixture should be thick enough to prevent them sinking. Slam it into the oven for 20 minutes on 220°C (425°F, Gas Mark 7).

FISH:

There's loads of ways to cook a fish
And here's a few that are 'delish'!

CHEESY FISH GRILL

This is a brilliant recipe and so easy, cheesy, peasy. So get into your kitchen and start making some for your mum – then again, on second thoughts, forget about your mum and start making it for yourself.

Shopping:

Butter   3 oz cheese
4 cod/haddock fillets   1 teaspoon mustard powder
1 onion   Salt and pepper

Wipe the grill with butter to stop the fish from sticking. You can use any type of fish for this, just whack the steaks under a medium grill, to start cooking. Chop the onion and grate the cheese. Mix them together with the mustard, salt, pepper and a knob of butter. Squidge it all up – terribly tactile stuff. Turn over the fish and dollop the mixture on top of each portion and push back under the grill. Leave for 5 minutes or so for the onion to cook and the cheese to melt down over the fish.

SLASHED FISH WITH YOGHURT AND SPICES

It's completely amazing what you can get your fishmonger to do for you, by way of filleting and preparing fish. This dish is quick and simple and totally delicious.

Shopping:

2 white flatfish, filleted
Yoghurt
Garlic powder

Coriander
Chilli powder
Lemon juice

Unless you are very clever, buy your fish filleted. Wash it and slash with deep diagonal slits – this is so that all the sauce goes into the fish when cooking. Pour the yoghurt into a bowl and add a little garlic, coriander and chilli powder – about a teaspoon of each, as it shouldn't be too spicy. Squeeze the lemon into the yoghurt and mix. Put the fish into an ovenproof dish and cover with half the sauce. Place under a hot grill for 7–8 minutes, then turn the fish over and pour over the rest of the sauce. Grill for a further 7–8 minutes.

FISH IN BREADCRUMBS

Any kind of fish will do, but dabs are very cheap and greatly underrated.

Shopping:
1 lb dabs, filleted
Flour
2 eggs
Stale bread
Salt and pepper
Oil

Sauce:
Butter
Garlic

Ask your fishmonger to fillet the fish for you. Lay out 3 bowls containing seasoned flour, beaten egg and lots of breadcrumbs. You can make your own breadcrumbs by lightly toasting some bread and then crushing it in a bag with a rolling pin. Dip the fish in the flour, eggwash, salt and pepper and then coat in breadcrumbs. Heat the oil and fry the fish for about 3 minutes on each side until it is golden brown.

Peel and chop some garlic. Melt some butter over the heat and add the garlic. Pour the garlic butter over the fried fish.

BLACKENED FISH

The fish needs to be very fresh, but cooks very quickly. You need a good oven-hood for this as it makes a lot of smoke. The Gremolata Garnish is brilliant, easy to do and great with any fish.

Shopping:

2 pieces white fish, filleted
Salt and pepper
Flour
Olive oil

Gremolata Garnish:
Parsley
Garlic
Lemon rind

Heat up the frying-pan so it's really hot, you don't need any oil. Take your fillet of fish, season, sprinkle lightly with flour and coat in a little olive oil. Put into the pan and fry on each side for about 30 seconds – there will be clouds of smoke, but this fierce heat should be enough to cook the fish.

Finely chop your parsley and garlic, grate the lemon rind and mix together to make the garnish. Sprinkle it on to the fish.

FISH STEW

If you tell your fishmonger what you are making, he should give you a selection of different types of fish according to the season and this will give a nice variation in flavours. If he won't, go and find a better fishmonger!

Shopping:

2 lb fish, filleted
1 onion
Garlic
1 yellow pepper
Olive oil

1 tin tomatoes
Tomato purée
Salt and pepper
White wine

Wash the fish, dry it, and then chop it into bite-sized chunks. Chop the onion, garlic and pepper. Heat the oil in a pan and add the onion, and after a few minutes, the fish and garlic. Reduce the heat, as the fish cooks very quickly. Add the tomatoes, tomato purée and seasoning. Cook for a while then add a touch of white wine to finish off.

POACHED FISH

*Poaching times for fish vary, but they can be very brief –
give it a prod with a knife to see if it's cooked. Any white
fish will cook well this way.*

Shopping:

2 pieces fish, filleted
1 small onion
White wine
Herbs

Sauce:
Few mushrooms
1 small carton double
    cream
Butter
Pepper

Get your fishmonger to fillet the fish for you. Chop the
onion and slice the mushrooms. Put enough white wine
in a saucepan to cover the bottom and then fold over the
fish and place in the wine. Sprinkle herbs on top together
with a little chopped onion. Too much onion detracts
from the flavour of the fish. Poach for about 5 minutes.
Remove the fish, cover in foil and place under the grill to
keep it warm.

Put the wine back on the heat, add the sliced
mushrooms, the rest of the onions and reduce the wine.
When the onions and mushrooms are tender, add the
double cream and a little bit of butter and stir until the
sauce thickens. Grind in some pepper to taste, place the
fish on the plates and pour the sauce over the fish.

MACKEREL IN GARLIC AND OLIVE OIL

When buying fish look for two things: a clear eye and a smooth and shiny skin – this means the fish is fresh.

Shopping:

2 mackerel, cleaned and
gutted
Olive oil

Garlic
Dried rosemary
Salt and pepper

Give your fish a good rinse. Heat a good dollop of oil in a frying-pan, chop the garlic roughly and add to the pan with some rosemary. Sprinkle salt and pepper over the fish, then add to the pan and baste with the oil. Put some foil loosely over the top of the frying-pan and put into the oven for 20 minutes at 150°C (300°F, Gas Mark 2) – make sure the handle of the frying-pan is heatproof. It will come out lovely and succulent, but don't serve the garlic pieces with the fish if they're very brown as they will taste bitter.

FISH IN A PARCEL

You can use red fish such as sea bream for this, or any white fish. Don't forget to ask your fishmonger to skin and bone it for you.

Shopping:

½ lb fish, filleted
Bunch spring onions
1 piece ginger

Salt and pepper
1 dessertspoon soy sauce
Butter/margarine

Wash the fish and cut the piece in half so that you have 2 portions. Finely chop the spring onions and ginger – not too much of this or it will overpower the fish. Tear off 2 large rectangular pieces of foil and cut out a heart shape in each. Grease the foil lightly with oil and put a portion of fish on each one. Put a handful of onion and ginger over the fish and sprinkle with salt and pepper and add a dash of soy sauce. Fold over the foil and seal the edges with your fingers, leaving room around the fish. Place the bags on a baking tray and cook in the oven for 10 minutes at 190°C (375°F, Gas Mark 5) – the bags will puff up. Whiff the wonderful aroma when you cut through the foil to get to the cooked fish.

Mystery Chef comment:
'When the fishy bags have puffed,
that's the time to feel real chuffed.'

FISH FLAN

Pilchards? They may sound disgusting, but in actual fact they are highly yummy, incredibly healthy and extraordinarily cheap.

Shopping:

1 packet shortcrust pastry	Few mushrooms
Butter/margarine	1 tin pilchards
2 eggs	Salt and pepper
1 tin evaporated milk	Cheese

Roll out the pastry – the quick, convenience packet stuff – and lay it in a greased flan dish. Press it down around the flan dish and trim off the edges. Break the eggs into a bowl and whisk together with a third of a pint of evaporated milk. Chop up the mushrooms and open the tin of pilchards. Mix these in with the egg, add salt and pepper and pour into the flan case. Sprinkle grated cheese on top and cook in the oven for 20 minutes at 200°C (400°F, Gas Mark 6).

MOULES MARINIÈRE

It is important to clean mussels properly. Scrape the mussels with the back of a knife to get rid of all the barnacles, then carefully pull out the beards – or anything else that's sticking out between the shells – with your fingers. Run all the mussels under cold water and knock them around – this will make them spit out the sand inside. You can tell if a mussel is bad because when it is uncooked it will spring back again if you press the shells together. If a mussel doesn't open up when cooked, it means it's dead and should not be eaten – you should never have to prise open a mussel when cooked.

Shopping:

1 lb mussels	Thyme
1 leek	2 bay leaves
1 onion	White wine
2 cloves garlic	$\frac{1}{4}$ pint double cream
Butter	Parsley

Having cleaned the mussels properly, chop the onion, garlic and leek very finely and fry in butter. Add thyme and a couple of bay leaves. Then put the mussels into the frying-pan with a good splash of white wine and cook for about 5 minutes. Turn the mussels over as they are boiling to check for dead ones – these will make you very queasy if you eat them. Add the cream to the sauce and bring back to the boil. Serve with parsley and you can eat as many as you like because they're not fattening!

STUFFED SPRATS

This is good fun if you enjoy pulling out fish intestines for quarter of an hour.

Shopping:

16 sprats	Flour
1 packet Boursin cheese	Oil
2 eggs	

Wash the sprats and, just to make sure they are dead, cut off the heads. Slice the fish down the belly, pull out the intestines, push down on the backbone and then pull it out. Wash again and stuff each sprat with Boursin cheese and fold the belly flaps back together. Beat the eggs and dip the fish into the egg and then coat in flour. Fry in hot oil for 3–4 minutes on each side.

PRAWN PROVENÇALE

Get your fishmonger to show you how to peel a prawn, or cheat and buy them ready-shelled in frozen packets. Either way, this is simply 'prawnographic'.

Shopping:

¾ lb prawns	2-3 tomatoes
1 onion	Parsley
Garlic	White wine
Butter	

Peel the prawns – take off the head, remove the eggy inside bit and the rest of the shell – so you're left with the nice stuff. Chop the onions and crush the garlic and fry in a knob of butter. Add the sliced tomatoes, chopped parsley and a good splashing of white wine. Cook for 5–6 minutes, then add the peeled prawns. Cook these for 2–3 minutes, then serve with pasta or rice.

YOUR FISHMONGER WILL DO **ANYTHING** IF YOU ASK HIM...

What a TWIT!

FISH MONGER

...ALMOST...

CARNIVOROUS:

You don't have to be well off,
To be a mega-meaty toff.

BEEF SENSATION

If you are simply filthy rich you can use fillet steak for this, but if you are broke and want to impress someone with a real dinner party meal, use braising steak.

Shopping:

Oil
Butter
1 onion
1 green pepper
Garlic
1 medium piece braising steak
1 tin tomatoes

Tomato purée
Worcester sauce
Tabasco sauce
Basil
Black pepper
English mustard
Brown sugar

Heat a little oil and butter in the frying-pan together – the oil stops the butter burning and the butter gives it a richer taste. Chop the onion, garlic, pepper and cut the braising steak into bite-sized chunks. Fry the onion until it goes translucent, then add the garlic, pepper and the pieces of braising steak. When the meat is brown, add the tomatoes, a squirt of tomato purée, Worcester sauce, Tabasco, basil and black pepper. Follow this up with the English mustard and brown sugar. Pour this mixture into an ovenproof dish – don't ruin your mother's plastic saucepan handles by putting them in the oven. Cover the dish with foil and cook for about $1\frac{1}{2}$ hours at 180°C (350°F, Gas Mark 4). This dish also re-heats well.

STEAK WITH MUSHROOM AND WALNUT SAUCE

Spoil yourself, save up for weeks and eat this expensive restaurant nosh for a treat. You can get fairly cheap frying steak from the supermarket though, so it needn't break the bank.

Mystery Chef hygiene tip:
'Always remember to wash those handies after touching uncooked meat as you could give yourself a nasty turn if you don't.'

Shopping:

1 onion
Butter
Oil
Mushrooms
Garlic
White wine

Mixed herbs
Salt and pepper
Walnuts
1 largish piece braising steak
1 small carton single cream

Chop the onion roughly and fry in melted butter in a saucepan. Add the chopped mushrooms and crushed garlic. Pour in some white wine – whatever you've got left after drinking it all – add the herbs, salt and crushed walnuts. Allow to simmer for a while so the mixture is reduced as the alcohol evaporates. Add the cream to the mushroom mixture and boil until the sauce begins to thicken. Meanwhile sprinkle the steak with mixed herbs and black pepper. Fry the steak in butter and oil, turning to cook on both sides. Pour over the sauce and serve.

STEAK AND KIDNEY PUDDING

A time-honoured favourite that can't be beat. Traditionally oysters were added too – we can't afford them.

Shopping:

¾ lb chuck steak
¼ lb ox kidney
½ onion
3 oz mushrooms
Mushroom ketchup/
   Worcester sauce
Thyme
1 bay leaf
Parsley
Salt and pepper

¾ tablespoon flour
Butter/margarine
1 beef stock cube

Suet crust:
6 oz self-raising flour
Pinch of baking powder
3 oz suet
Thyme
Salt and pepper

Dice the chuck steak and ox kidney, cutting out the sinews and fat. Chop the onion and quarter the mushrooms. Put all the prepared ingredients into a bowl and add a sprinkling of thyme, parsley, the bay leaf, salt, pepper and a splash of ketchup. Add the flour to soak up the fat from the meat.

In another bowl make the suet crust. Mix the flour, baking powder and suet with enough cold water to form a dough. Add the herbs and seasoning and roll out on a floured surface. Grease a deep heatproof basin with butter and then line it with two thirds of the suet mixture, pressing it against the sides. Fill the basin with the meat so it's about three-quarters full. Top up with water or half a pint of beef stock and put the remaining suet dough over the top to form a lid and trim off the excess. Put foil loosely over the top of the basin and tie tightly with string to prevent water getting in while it's cooking. Place the bowl in simmering water in a saucepan and cook for 3–3½ hours, topping up the water as it evaporates – ideally the bowl should stand on a rack, above the heat, in the simmering water. Turn the pudding out.

COTTAGE PIE

Q: What's the difference between a cottage pie and a shepherd's pie?
A: Cottage pie is made with minced beef and shepherd's pie is made with minced lamb.

Shopping:

Oil
1 lb minced beef
2 small onions
1 large carrot
Mushrooms
Salt and pepper

Mixed herbs
1 pint boiling water
3–4 old potatoes
Butter
Milk
4 teaspoons gravy granules

Heat the oil in a frying-pan or large saucepan and, stirring continuously, brown the meat. Add the chopped onion, carrot and mushrooms to the pan. Sprinkle in the salt, pepper and herbs and pour in the boiling water. Simmer for 20 minutes. Meanwhile, peel and cut up the potatoes and put them in a pan of cold, salted water. Bring to the boil and simmer for 20 minutes. When the meat mixture is ready, drain the liquid into a bowl and spoon the meat into a casserole dish. Drain the potatoes and mash with butter, milk, salt and pepper. Spread the mash over the meat and put in the oven for 30 minutes at 180°C (350°F, Gas Mark 4). Heat the liquid from the meat and add the gravy granules. Serve the gravy with the Cottage Pie.

CORNED BEEF HASH

Like tuna fish, a tin of corned beef is something you should always have in your larder. Fresh corned beef from a butcher is cheaper, but you could use tinned for this recipe.

Shopping:

Corned beef   Potatoes
1 onion   Salt and pepper
Oil

Chop up the meat and onion and fry the onion in hot oil. Meanwhile peel the potatoes, cut into pieces and parboil for about 10 minutes; then drain and add to the frying-pan. Finally add the chopped corned beef and cook on until it's hot and crumbly. Season and serve with boiled cabbage and tomato ketchup. This is the ultimate in grub that's cheap, easy, quick and tasty.

VEAL STROGANOFF

Veal is calf's meat and tends to be expensive, but you can use pork for this recipe instead. If you are using pork, make sure it's properly cooked by taking a bit out of the pan and cutting it in half to make sure it's white not pink.

Shopping:

4 veal escalopes
Butter
1 onion
6 oz mushrooms
Garlic

Tomato purée
Plain flour
1 carton fresh sour cream
Salt and pepper
Lemon juice

Beat the escalopes with a rolling pin until they are thin and cut them into short strips. Chop the onion, mushrooms and garlic and fry in melted butter. When the onion goes translucent, add the tomato purée and a little flour to thicken up the sauce. Cook for 2–3 minutes, stirring all the time. Melt some butter in a separate pan, add the veal and fry until it's browned on both sides. Add the meat to the sauce and then stir in the cream, lemon juice, salt and pepper. Heat through without letting it boil.

44

HONEYED PORK CHOPS

It is important to make sure that the pork is properly cooked – make a little cut with a knife when you think the chops are ready. Grilling chops with honey is an exciting alternative to the usual apple sauce.

Shopping:

2 pork chops
Honey
Oregano
Olive oil
2 courgettes

1 onion
1 red pepper
Mushrooms
Garlic

Glaze the chops with honey and sprinkle with oregano on both sides before putting under a medium grill. Chop the courgettes, onion, pepper, mushrooms and garlic and fry them all in oil in a pre-heated frying-pan. Take the pork chops out from under the grill and serve with the vegetables.

Yum!

PORK CASSEROLE

This is a one pot survival meal so you can save on the washing up. Chopping up the meat is easy, just take all the meaty bits away from all the fatty, gristly and skinny bits with a sharp knife!

Shopping:

2 pork chops/belly pork
  slices
Flour
Salt and pepper
Butter

1 onion
Mushrooms
1 stock cube
Cider (optional)
1–2 potatoes

Chop the belly pork or pork chops into bite-sized pieces. Chuck a bit of flour on to a plate and season. Coat the pork in the flour and fry in melted butter. Chop the onion and mushrooms and add to the pork in the pan. Fry for a few minutes, then stir in your leftover flour, which will help to thicken the sauce. Pour boiling water over the stock cube and stir into the mixture in the frying-pan. Add a bit of cider if you've got any lurking in the fridge and simmer for 20 minutes. Peel and roughly chop the potatoes into chunks, add to the pan and simmer for a further 15 minutes.

POTÉE AUVERGNATE

A traditional French stew, slightly adapted. The flavours of the boiling pork and the smoked bacon offset well and improve the dish.

Shopping:

$\frac{1}{2}$ lb pork belly slice, smoked
2 pieces shoulder of pork
2 carrots
1 leek
1 turnip
$\frac{1}{2}$ cabbage

1 onion
2 cloves
Garlic
Salt and pepper
Bouquet garni
2 medium potatoes

Simmer the bacon and shoulder of pork in plenty of water for 1 hour. Peel and cut all the vegetables into large chunks, except the onion. Cut the onion in half and stick 1 clove into each piece. Add all the vegetables to the simmering water with the meat plus the chopped garlic, salt, pepper and bouquet garni. Peel the potatoes and chop into chunks. When the meat is cooked, add the potatoes and boil for another 15 minutes, or until the potatoes are soft. Spoon it all out on to a plate.

HAM AND MUSHROOM CRUMBLE

The magic of this is that there are no mushrooms in it, just condensed mushroom soup – amazing! You can get cheap off-cuts of ham from your butcher which are great for a crumble because you can't see what funny shapes you are eating anyway.

Shopping:

1 onion
Margarine
$\frac{3}{4}$ lb ham
1 tin condensed mushroom
  soup

1 tin sweetcorn
1 packet breadcrumbs
Cheese

Chop and fry the onion in margarine. Chop up the ham into little pieces and add to the pan with the soup and sweetcorn. Stir it in and heat for a few minutes. Put into a casserole dish. Mix your breadcrumbs (you can make these yourself by toasting some stale bread then beating it with a rolling pin... preferably in a plastic bag) and grated cheese, and sprinkle on top. Into the oven for 45 minutes at 180°C (350°F, Gas Mark 4) and it's nice 'n' crispy on top.

HAM AND LEEKS

If you buy a pack of convenience cheese sauce for this dish, it will take you no time at all to make, it will be lump-free and your friends will think that you're a brilliant cook.

Shopping:

2 leeks
Ham slices
Salt
Cheese sauce mix

Milk
Butter/margarine
Cheese

Top and tail the leeks and cut each leek into 2–3 pieces. Place the leeks in boiling, salted water for 10 minutes. For the cheese sauce you can read the instructions on the back of the packet – if you can read. In case you can't, put the cheese sauce mix in a saucepan and add milk, blending it with a spoon as you bring it to the boil. When the leeks are cooked, drain them off and wrap each one in a ham slice and place in a greased ovenproof dish. Pour the cheese sauce over the top and then sprinkle with grated cheese. Shove it in the oven for 15 minutes at 180°C (350°F, Gas Mark 4).

BEANY PIE

*This is an up-market version of sausage and beans –
sausagemeat is cheaper than sausages though.*

Mystery Chef declaration:
'If you wanna be faster on your feet, eat beany
pie and you'll float down the street.'

Shopping:

Flour
Butter/margarine
1 packet pastry

1 lb sausagemeat
2 large tins baked beans

Flour the surface and roll out the pastry. Grease an oven
dish and line with half the pastry, trimming off the
excess. Squidge out the sausagemeat and spread on to
the pastry. Open the beans and pour on top of the
sausagemeat. Lay the rest of the pastry over the top and
press down at the edges, to make a lid. Cook in the oven

BLATT.

ZOOM!!

TOAD IN THE HOLE

Why is this called Toad in the Hole when there is no toad and no hole?

Shopping:

Butter/margarine
4-8 sausages
4 oz plain flour

Pinch of salt
1 egg
$\frac{1}{2}$ pint milk

Grease a roasting tin with butter and prick the sausages. Put them into the tin and cook in a pre-heated oven for 10 minutes at 180°C (350°F, Gas Mark 4), so they are half cooked. Meanwhile sift the flour and salt, and mix in the egg. Gradually add the milk and keep beating until the batter is smooth. Take the sausages out of the oven and pour the batter into the hot baking tray over the sausages. Put back into the oven and cook for 15 minutes, then at a lower heat for a further 10 minutes.

SAUSAGE BAKE

'Sausage bake is a piece of cake.
No, it's not, it's sausage bake.'

Shopping:

1 onion
1 cooking apple
4 sausages
Butter
Milk

Plain flour
Cheese
Salt and pepper
Basil

Chop the onion and grate the apple. Place the sausages and chopped onion in a greased ovenproof dish and cover with the apple. Heat some butter in a saucepan and add the milk, stirring until it comes to the boil. Remove from the heat and slowly add the flour to the saucepan. Pile in the grated cheese, salt and pepper and basil, put back on the heat and stir until it thickens. This is just an alternative way of making a roux sauce. Pour the sauce over the sausages, covering them and wham it in the oven for 45 minutes at 200°C (400°F, Gas Mark 6).

TINNED FRANKFURTER CASSEROLE

*This is a great meal from store-cupboard stand bys,
'cause most of the ingredients are in tins.*

Shopping:

1 onion
Mushrooms
1 tin frankfurters
1 tin sweetcorn
1 tin tomatoes
1 tin kidney beans

1 tin baked beans
1 tin condensed tomato
  soup
4 rashers bacon
Oil

Chop the onion and mushrooms – it's fungus time! Open all the tins and pour away the juice from the frankfurters, kidney beans and sweetcorn. Cut the bacon and frankfurters into pieces. Heat the oil in a pan and add the onion, mushroom, bacon and frankfurters, 5 minutes later, pour them into a casserole dish, chuck in the rest of the ingredients and stir it all around. If it's not juicy enough add some more water. Cook in the oven for 1 hour at 180°C (350°F, Gas Mark 4).

ALMOST TRENDY ADVERT HAIRCUT

AWFUL TOOTHY ADVERT GRIN.

HEY KIDS DONT BE AFRAID TO OPEN A TIN!

feeds an army!

SUPER TINNED FRANKFUR YUM YUM

MAKING IT OBVIOUS!

LAMB MEDALLIONS

'Medallions' is just a fancy way of trimming meat off the bone. It's the sort of thing you would get in a restaurant, but the breadcrumb coating and sauce can be adapted to home cookery. It's a neat way of making chops look really sexy by whopping on mustard and herby things.

Shopping:

1 lamb loin chop
Butter
Dijon mustard
Breadcrumbs
Salt and pepper
Mixed herbs

Sauce:
Orange juice
Redcurrant jelly

Get your butcher to cut your loin chop in half. Run a knife around the bone and trim off the rest of the fat, so you are left with a round medallion of meat with a spike of bone. Spread a knob of butter on each side and mustard on top. Make your own breadcrumbs by grating slightly stale bread, and mix in salt, pepper and herbs. Cover the medallion with the breadcrumbs and place under the grill. Cook for about 10 minutes on each side, depending on how you like your chops done.

To make the sauce, put 2–3 glugs of orange juice into a saucepan and spoon in enough redcurrant jelly to taste. Bubble for about 15 minutes until the liquid has reduced and thickened. Spoon over the medallions.

ROAST LAMB AND MINT SAUCE

This is a good old traditional Sunday lunch meal. It doesn't have to be expensive as you can get cheap cuts from your butcher and make some really cheap and easy mint sauce and gravy.

Shopping:
Garlic
Salt
Shoulder joint of lamb
Dried rosemary
Pepper

Mint Sauce:
Dried mint
White wine vinegar
Sugar

Gravy:
Flour
Marmite

Chop the garlic and mash it up with a fair bit of salt. The more salt you have, the better the crackling on the outside of the meat. Rub the mixture into the meat. Sprinkle rosemary and pepper on to the bottom of the lamb, as it won't burn on the underside but the herbs will still mix in with the juices to give extra flavour. Stick the lamb in a roasting tin and whack it into a pre-heated oven, around 200°C (400°F, Gas Mark 6) for $1\frac{1}{2}$ hours.

To make your mint sauce, sprinkle some chopped mint, fresh or dried, into a bowl and pour in enough wine vinegar to cover it. Add a little sugar to sweeten and allow to stand for a while for the mint to soak in the liquid.

When the lamb is ready, remove from the roasting tin and mix the juices in the tin with some flour and a bit of Marmite diluted with water to make your gravy.

LANCASHIRE HOT-POT

You can use a really cheap cut of lamb for this – you're going to cook it for ages anyway, and long cooking times make tough meat tender.

Shopping:

2 chump lamb chops	Butter
Oil	Tomato purée
1 onion	2 bay leaves
2 carrots	Thyme
Garlic	1 stock cube
1 leek	2 potatoes

Trim the lamb, removing most of the fat and cut into chunks. Leave a bit of fat on to give it extra flavour. Brown the lamb in hot oil for 5 minutes in a frying-pan. Peel and slice the carrots and leek, chop the onion and garlic and add to the lamb. Fry until the vegetables are soft, adding a little butter if it becomes too dry. Add the thyme, bay leaves and half a pint of stock, with a squirt of tomato purée. Stir, and simmer for a few minutes before spooning it into an ovenproof dish. Peel the potatoes and cut them into wafer-thin slices – layer on top of the lamb and vegetables. Brush the potatoes with melted butter and slam the lamb in the oven for $1\frac{1}{4}$ hours at 180°C (350°F, Gas Mark 4) or lower the temperature and extend the cooking time.

PEANUT CHICKEN

You can grill, kebab or barbecue the chicken for this – just make sure it's cooked through properly before you eat it. The peanut satay sauce is delicious, but go easy on the salt as the peanut butter already contains plenty.

Shopping:

$\frac{3}{4}$ lb chicken breasts, boned
1 large onion
Garlic
Oil

Peanut butter
Lemon juice
Soy sauce
Salt and pepper
Curry powder

Cut the chicken into bite-sized pieces. Finely chop the onion and garlic and fry in hot oil for a few minutes. Add about half the jar of peanut butter, the juice of half a lemon and the other ingredients. Add enough water to make a smooth paste and simmer. Fry the chicken pieces in a little oil in a separate pan. When the chicken is cooked, serve and pour over the sauce. It's ready to eat.

OYAKO DOMBORI

A Japanese-style, spicy chicken omelette thing – quite expensive, but well worth knowing about. Dashi is a sort of Japanese fish stock, but you can buy the equivalent of an Oxo cube in the form of dashi powder from oriental specialist shops. The nori seaweed is a sort of garnish, used much as we'd use parsley. It's delicious.

Shopping:

Japanese/short-grain rice
2 small chicken breasts, skinned and boned
1 onion
½ pint water

3 tablespoons soy sauce
1 tablespoon dashi
2 eggs
1 sheet nori seaweed

Wash the rice before boiling it, cook for as long as it says on the packet. Cut the chicken into small pieces and finely chop the onion. Pour the water into a bowl, add the soy sauce, the dashi and stir to dissolve. Put a little of the dashi liquid into the saucepan and boil the onion in this for about 2 minutes, until the stock has almost evaporated. Add the chicken and beaten egg to the onion, stir once, then leave for a couple of minutes with the lid on for the egg to set. Spoon the rice out on to plates and place the Oyako Dombori on top. Take the seaweed sheet and pass over a hot ring two or three times – it should then be lightly toasted and will easily crush in your hand. Crumble it over the chickeny-egg as a garnish.

CHICKEN CACCIATORE

This means 'Huntsman's chicken'. It is not the traditional recipe but a bed-sit variant. So, 'cover yourself in glory, cook Chicken Cacciatore'.

Shopping:

1 onion	Mushrooms
Garlic	1 tin tomatoes
Oil	Salt and pepper
2 chicken breasts,	Mixed herbs
skinned and boned	Parsley
1 green pepper	White wine

Chop the onion and garlic and fry in oil. The easy way to prepare garlic is to crush it first with the back of a knife, remove the loose skin, and then chop. Make 2–3 cuts in the top of the chicken so it looks as if it's been hunted and then put into the pan to brown on both sides. Meanwhile slice the pepper and mushrooms. Put them in a bowl with the tomatoes, seasoning, herbs and parsley and mix with a fork. Put the chicken into a casserole dish, spoon the onions over the top and then pour on the sauce. Dash in some white wine and cover with a lid or foil. Cook for 45 minutes at 180°C (350°F, Gas Mark 4). Cook for longer than this if you are using more chicken.

59

EASY CHICKEN CASSEROLE

As easy as laying an egg and more fun to do! Did you know that you don't have to take hours to pierce that seal on a tube of tomato purée 'cause there's a spiky bit on the top of the lid! The only thing is, if you do it the proper way, it doesn't squirt everywhere.

Shopping:

2 large chicken portions
Chicken seasoning
Salt and pepper
Oil
1 onion

$\frac{3}{4}$ lb mushrooms
1 tin condensed mushroom
   soup
Tomato purée

Wash the chicken and sprinkle over a little chicken seasoning, salt and pepper. Brown the chicken on both sides in the oil. Chop the onion and mushrooms and then add these to the pan. Fry for 10 minutes, then pour in the soup to make a good creamy sauce together with a squirt of tomato purée. Simmer for about 45 minutes on the hob, with the pan covered, and add some water if the sauce becomes dry.

COQ AU VIN

Have a finger-lickin' good time and compare the size of those chicken thighs, guys!

Shopping:

1 onion
Garlic
2 carrots
Mushrooms
Oil
Flour

Dried tarragon
Salt and pepper
4-6 chicken thighs
Red wine
Cornflour

Chop the onion, garlic, carrots and mushrooms. Fry the onion and garlic in hot oil, then add the rest of the vegetables. Leave for 5 minutes until they are partially cooked and spoon into a casserole dish. Mix the flour, tarragon, salt and pepper and coat the chicken. Add the chicken to the casserole dish and pour over excessive amounts of red wine. Put on the hob to simmer for 45 minutes – the alcohol will evaporate and leave you with a rich flavoured sauce. Add some chicken stock if the casserole becomes dry and some cornflour or thickener if the sauce is too watery.

QUICK CHICKEN SUPREME

Don't be afraid of using a pressure cooker – it won't blow your house to pieces if you do it properly! You can make this recipe if you don't have a pressure cooker, it just takes a little longer.

Daft warning: some people call their chicken silly names like Cedric - if you are cool, you call it Esmerelda.

Shopping:

1 medium chicken
Salt and pepper
Butter
Plain flour
2 pints milk
Garlic

1 lb mushrooms
1 lb onions
Lard/oil
1 packet frozen sweetcorn
1 packet quick rice, cooked
Parsley

Clean and prepare the chicken. Put a bit of water in the pressure cooker and place the chicken on top of the metal rack above the water. Season the chicken with salt and pepper and leave to cook – 30 minutes should be enough. Melt the butter in a large casserole dish, add flour and seasoning and stir into a paste. Add the milk slowly and then the crushed garlic, by now you should have a thick sauce. Chop the mushrooms and onions and fry in melted lard or oil. Defrost the sweetcorn. Remove the chicken from the pressure cooker – it should be as tender as if it had been in the oven for 2 hours. Slice the chicken into pieces, removing it from the bone and add everything to the white sauce – Cedric, sweetcorn, onions and mushrooms. This can be eaten straight away with rice and garnished with parsley or put into the oven for 40–60 minutes at 180°C (350°F, Gas Mark 4). You can use a cold leftover chicken for this dish.

DONT WORRY ABOUT THE AMOUNT OF MUSTARD.
(UNLESS YOU'RE A RABBIT)

MUSTARD RABBIT

You can cook a mustardy bunny, chicken, pork . . .
Dollops of mustard used like this may seem alarming,
but it loses it's strength in the cooking.

Shopping:

2–3 rabbit portions
3 tablespoons English
  mustard
1 tablespoon oil

Sauce:
1 carton single cream
Salt and pepper

Wash the rabbit and pat dry with a kitchen towel. Mix together the mustard and oil and then smear it excessively all over the rabbit. Put the rabbit into an ovenproof dish and put into a really hot oven, turning it down to about 180°C (350°F, Gas Mark 4). Cook for about 50 minutes then remove the rabbit from the dish on to a hotplate.

Pour the cream into the juices left in the dish, add salt and pepper, and stir round on the heat. Pour the sauce over the rabbit.

OFFAL:

Don't listen to high table waffle,
Go and cook yourself some offal.

STUFFED LAMBS' HEARTS

Offal is hugely underrated in this country, but it's cheap and this recipe is delicious.

Shopping:

2 lambs' hearts	Garlic
1 onion	Flour
$\frac{1}{4}$ lb sausagemeat	1 tin draught Guinness
1 tin stoned prunes	1 bay leaf
Salt and pepper	Parsley

Cut off the top of the lambs' hearts so you can get to the cavities. Chop the onion and place half of it in a bowl with the sausagemeat, stoned prunes and seasoning. Mix all of these together and press the stuffing firmly into the spaces in the hearts. Next, carefully brown the hearts in a frying-pan, making sure the stuffing doesn't fall out. Then put the rest of the chopped onion and garlic into the frying-pan with the hearts and turn the lambs' hearts on end so the stuffing stays in. Sprinkle flour over the onions, to soak up the fat and help make the sauce. Pour in half the can of Guinness and a bit of water and add the bay leaf. Put foil over the top and put in the oven for about 1 hour. Remove the hearts and slice into about 3 pieces. Season the sauce, pour over the hearts and garnish with parsley.

LAMBS' KIDNEYS

There tends to be a real stigma about buying stuff in butcher's and fishmonger's, but they should be really helpful – if not, go and find one that is.

Shopping:

4 lambs' kidneys
Butter
$\frac{1}{4}$ pint single cream
1 teaspoon honey

1 teaspoon wholegrain
 mustard
Salt and pepper
Rice, cooked

The fatty globule inside the kidney is not very tasty and should be removed. Cut each kidney in half and snip out this bit with a pair of scissors or a small sharp knife and cut the kidneys into bite-sized pieces. Melt the butter in the frying-pan and chuck the kidneys in when the butter starts to sizzle. Just seal the outside so the colour changes from dark pink to a light browny-pink. Then add the cream (stirring all the time), honey, mustard, salt and pepper and bring to the boil. Turn down the heat and simmer gently for 5–10 minutes, depending on how well cooked you like your kidneys – most people overcook them which makes them tough – ideally they should be slightly pink in the middle. Serve with cooked rice.

LIVER AND ONIONS

Calf's liver is very fine but a bit on the expensive side, lamb's liver is a lot cheaper. If you don't overcook liver it won't taste like that rubbery stuff you had at school. Ask your butcher to slice it thinly for you and it will only take a couple of minutes to cook on each side.

Shopping:

2 onions
Oil
Salt and pepper
Butter
Sugar

White wine vinegar/stock
1 lb calf's/lamb's liver
Flour
Parsley

Peel and slice the onions and fry them in hot oil. Add salt, pepper, a knob of butter and a sprinkling of sugar and stir. Add a little wine vinegar and a bit more butter, and it should thicken into a nice sauce. Cover the liver in flour, shake off any excess and fry in hot oil. Flip it over when it begins to brown. Don't overcook your liver. Remove the liver, cover in the sauce and sprinkle some chopped parsley on top.

TRIPE IN BREADCRUMBS

Tripe is the prepared (i.e. cleaned and boiled) yucky bits of farmyard animals and looks like your granny's swimming hat. It's relatively cheap and old people have a taste for it – it's certainly an acquired taste. Tripe stalls sell it cold and ready for eating and it's like the ham gristle you would usually spit out. However, tripe is a delicacy in France – give this a try.

Shopping:

1 lb tripe
Plain flour
1 egg
Breadcrumbs
Oil

Sauce:
6 oz butter
Capers
Lemon juice
Parsley

Cut the tripe into chunks, 1 inch square, and dust in the flour. Dip each piece into the whisked egg and then cover in breadcrumbs. Fry in hot oil until it is crispy and golden – and completely disguised!

To make the sauce, melt the butter and add the capers and lemon juice. Keep it bubbling vigorously. The capers are sharp and vinegary and offset the other flavours. Cover the tripe in the sauce and sprinkle with freshly chopped parsley.

MINUTES LATER... IT'S COOKED!

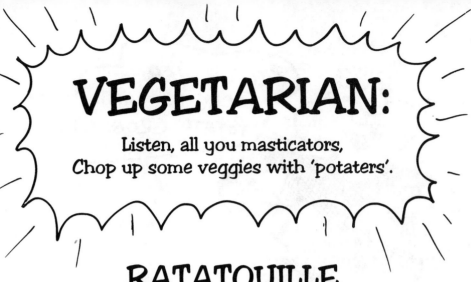

VEGETARIAN:

Listen, all you masticators,
Chop up some veggies with 'potaters'.

RATATOUILLE

If you want to find out how to cook proper ratatouille, look in your dictionary between 'ratbag' and 'rat-a-tat'. If you don't mind eating greasy aubergines this is a really groovy meal and you can use up all those vegetables that are in danger of going mouldy in your fridge.

Shopping:
Olive oil
2 aubergines
Mushrooms
2–3 courgettes
1 onion
1 green pepper
Garlic

1 tin tomatoes
Tomato purée
Salt and pepper
Herbs
Sugar
Chilli powder

Wash the vegetables and start slicing the aubergines, then cut each slice into quarters. Heat the oil in a frying-pan, you need quite a bit as the aubergines tend to soak it all up. While the aubergines are cooking, chop up the mushrooms, courgettes, onion and green pepper. Add these to the frying-pan with the crushed garlic. Then add the tin of tomatoes, tomato purée, salt, pepper, herbs and a little sugar (sugar takes away the acidity of the tomatoes) – not forgetting the chilli. Simmer for about 30 minutes on a low heat and your groovy ratatouille is ready to go.

POTATO AND BUTTER BEAN CROQUETTES

If you're buying dried pulses you must remember to soak them overnight.
'Fill your pockets with crunchy croquettes.'

Shopping:

1 packet butter beans
3–4 potatoes
Parsley
Sesame seeds
Butter/margarine

Sauce:
Oil

1 onion
Garlic
2 sticks celery
1 tin tomatoes
Tomato purée
Crunchy peanut butter
Salt and pepper
Red wine (optional)

70

Soak the butter beans overnight, then cook in boiling water for 40 minutes. Scrub the spuds, cut into pieces and boil for 20 minutes. Mash the pulses and potatoes together with chopped parsley and firm into balls. Dip them in sesame seeds to coat and then place on a greased baking tray and put into the oven for about 10 minutes at 180°C (350°F, Gas Mark 4).

While your croquettes are getting hot in the oven, make the sauce by frying chopped onion, garlic and celery. Add the tomatoes, purée and peanut butter to thicken and add seasoning. You can also add a glug of red wine if you've got some. Pour the sauce over the croquettes and they're ready to eat.

GREEN PIE

It's called green pie because it's just so green, man. You can use any veg that's green - broccoli, sprouts or cabbage and it tastes a lot nicer than some other things that are green, if you know what we mean!

Shopping:

1 packet split peas
3 large potatoes
Breadcrumbs
1 packet spinach, fresh or
    frozen

Oil
Cheese

Soak your dried split peas in water overnight, then boil them for 45 minutes. Scrub the potatoes, cut into pieces and boil for 20 minutes. Make your own breadcrumbs by putting some sliced bread into the oven for a few minutes and then crunching it into little pieces. Sling the spinach into a saucepan with a little oil and cook. Then mash the spinach, potatoes and split peas together. Grease a tin and dollop half the mixture into the tin. Grate masses of cheese on top and then spoon on the rest of the green splodge. Mix the breadcrumbs with some oil and cover the green goo. Put in the oven for 40 minutes at 180°C (350°F, Gas Mark 4).

SHETVPHERD'S PIE

TVP is that meat-alternative for vegetarians who like meat! It is made of soya, is full of protein and mega-cheap – so, go get some. You can also bung it into meaty stews to make them go further.

Shopping:

1 vegetable stock cube
Mixed herbs
Garlic
Beef-flavoured textured
    vegetable protein
4 potatoes
2 leeks

1 onion
Oil
Salt and pepper
Milk
1 egg
Vegetarian cheese

Add hot water to the stock cube and mix in the herbs and crushed garlic. Cover the TVP with some of this liquid and leave to soak for 30 minutes. Peel and boil the spuds. Chop the leeks and onion and fry in a little oil with salt and pepper. When the vegetables are tender, dollop into a greased casserole dish and fry the squidgy TVP in the same frying-pan for 5 minutes, so all the flavour from the leeks and onion comes out. Meanwhile, mash the potatoes with milk and a raw egg. Put a layer of TVP on top of the leek and onion mixture, then a layer of potato, and top it off with grated cheese. Put it into the oven for 20 minutes at 180°C (350°F, Gas Mark 4).

TVP CURRY

TVP is textured vegetable protein – it looks like dog food and it tastes like dog food – BUT if you do incredible things with it, such as marinating in curry powder and herbs, it can taste great. TVP is completely natural.

Shopping:

1 packet textured vegetable protein
1 vegetable stock cube
Mixed herbs
Garlic
Oil

1 onion
1 red pepper
Mushrooms
Sultanas
Curry powder
Rice, cooked

Soak the TVP in the hot stock, just enough to cover it, and also add the mixed herbs and crushed garlic. Leave this for 30 minutes. Chop the onion, red pepper and mushrooms and fry the onion and pepper for a few minutes. Then add the mushrooms, sultanas, loads of curry powder and the TVP, which should have soaked up all the liquid and gone squidgy. Mix and simmer for 20 minutes, adding more stock if the mixture begins to dry out. Serve with rice.

RISOTTO

This is a not your traditional risotto but something a bit different and extremely colourful – it's got lots of brightly coloured and pretty vegetables in it – wild! Cashew nuts are a very fashionable taste, but go easy with the salt as the nuts are already very salty.

Shopping:

1 onion
Garlic
Oil
6 oz brown rice
1 pint boiling water
2–3 sticks celery
Mushrooms

1 red/green pepper
1 tin kidney beans
Roasted cashew nuts
Soy sauce
Salt and pepper
Parsley

Chop the onion and garlic and fry in oil. Add the dry rice to the frying-pan and cook for a few moments before adding the boiling water. You need $1\frac{1}{2}$ times the amount of water to rice, but add the water gradually to allow the rice to soak it up. Simmer for 30 minutes. Meanwhile chop the celery, pepper and mushrooms, and fry in another frying-pan for a few minutes. Drain the kidney beans and add to the vegetable mixture with the cashews, salt and pepper and soy sauce. Add the risotto rice, stir in and garnish with chopped parsley.

COUSCOUS

Couscous is much underrated and it can be used to replace both rice and potatoes. It is a sort of semolinary stuff and a traditional Tunisian dish, but you don't have to go all the way there to get it! If you're in doubt about what to do with it, you'll usually find helpful instructions on the packet.

Shopping:

1 box couscous
1 large onion
1 small cauliflower
Broccoli
$\frac{1}{4}$ lb mushrooms

1 red pepper
Garlic
Oil
1 tin tomatoes
Dried stoned dates

Soak 1 cup of couscous in 2 cups of boiling water and leave to stand. Chop up all the vegetables, keeping back half the onion and half the pepper. Pour some oil in a frying-pan and add all the vegetables, cover with a lid to keep the flavour in and stir occasionally. Add the tomatoes and pieces of date when the veg begins to soften. Meanwhile fry the leftover onion and pepper in some oil in another pan, adding the couscous after a few minutes. Spoon the vegetable mixture over the couscous.

TOFU STIR FRY

Tofu is soya bean curd and you will usually find it in a box in a cooling cabinet. It has a rather bland, neutral taste, but when cooked with other things, picks up other flavours wonderfully. In appearance it looks a bit like a rubber pillow that has been maturing in the rain on a rubbish tip for a few hundred years or so. It even retains it's wobbliness when frazzled – what else can make that claim?

Shopping:

1 packet tofu
1 onion
Oil
1 tin tomatoes

1 tin pineapple chunks
Cashew nuts
1 dessertspoon cornflour
4 tablespoons soy sauce

Drain the water off the tofu and cut into cubes. Chop the onion. Fry the onion and tofu for 3 minutes in hot oil. Add the tomatoes and cook for a further 5 minutes. Drain the pineapple and add to the pan with the cashew nuts. Mix the cornflour into the soy sauce and pour over the tofu and vegetables. Stir until it is well thickened. Simmer for 2 minutes adding a splash of water if the sauce becomes too thick.

KONBU NO NIMONO

Konku is a black Japanese seaweed, you can also use Hijiki seaweed. This is well worth the effort of finding the ingredients.

Shopping:

1 packet Konbu seaweed	Oil
1 packet tofu	2 teaspoons sugar
1 carrot	Soy sauce

Wipe the sheets of seaweed with a damp cloth to clean – don't put it under the tap as it will lose all its flavour. Cut into 1 inch squares. Dice the tofu, peel and slice the carrot. Fry the tofu cubes in a little hot oil – lift it out when it's lightly browned and drain off the excess oil on kitchen paper. Pour some boiling water into a saucepan – enough to cover the bottom of the pan – add the seaweed and boil for 5 minutes. Add the tofu and carrot to the pan and sprinkle with sugar and a fair amount of soy sauce. Cook for about 10 minutes, then get those chopsticks going.

SUMMER SALAD

This gets really exciting if you add avocado. You can also liven it up with chopped, cooked bacon, anchovies and whatever else you've got lying around – lovely!

Shopping:

Lettuce
Tomatoes
Cucumber
Bunch spring onions
1 avocado

Dressing:
Olive oil
White wine vinegar
French mustard
Garlic
Salt and pepper

Top and tail the spring onions. Wash all the salad vegetables, chop them up and chuck into a big bowl. Peel the skin off the avocado, cut it in half and remove the stone. Then slice the flesh thinly. Toss into the bowl. Cover the avocado in lemon juice or it will go brown.

To make your dressing, mix 3 parts olive oil to 1 part vinegar, add crushed garlic, a dollop of French mustard, salt and pepper and whisk it all up until it goes creamy – pour over the salad.

GREEK SALAD

Feta cheese is made from sheep's milk by some nice Greek shepherd up in the mountains somewhere. The salad dressing is really tasty and will keep a while in the fridge.

Shopping:

Stale bread

Oil

Garlic salt

1 carrot

$\frac{1}{2}$ cucumber

Tomatoes

Bunch spring onions

1 red pepper

Lettuce

Feta cheese

Dressing:

Olive oil

Wine vinegar

French mustard

Salt and pepper

Mixed herbs

Cut the stale bread into cubes and fry in a little hot oil to make your croutons. Sprinkle garlic salt over the top. When it's browned drain off the excess oil on kitchen paper. Chop up the rest of the salad vegetables and dice the feta cheese. Put all the ingredients into a bowl and toss.

To make the salad dressing mix 3 parts olive oil to 1 part wine vinegar. Then add, to taste, the mustard, seasoning and herbs. Pour over the salad and finally add the croutons.

SPICY STUFF:

Chilli is my favourite, I eat it every day,
Stick it in a casserole and you'll be blown away.

PILAU RICE

'Tilda' is a trade-mark of a recommended rice you can currently buy, and ghee is Indian butter. You shouldn't have any trouble getting this lot from an ethnic shop.

Shopping:

Tilda rice
2 medium onions
Ginger
Garlic
Ghee

Salt
1 bay leaf
2 sticks cinnamon
4–5 cardamoms
Milk

Wash the rice. Chop your onions, garlic and ginger and fry in melted ghee to give the dish that proper Indian taste. Add a pinch of salt and when the onions are beginning to brown add the chopped bay leaf, cinnamon and crushed cardamom pods. Pour in a little milk and leave to cook for 1 minute. Then add the dried rice and water – you need 1 cup of water to every cup of rice. Put the lid on and let the water evaporate. When the rice is done, put the saucepan (check the handle is heatproof) in a pre-heated oven for 5 minutes. You can add few drops of food colouring for that professional Indian restaurant look – but not too much! There's a bit of a knack to getting the rice right... but it's worth the effort.

CHICKEN KORMA

'This one's a real stormer,
Fantastic Chicken Korma,
You'll never get a trauma
If you eat Chicken Korma.'

This is a delicate dish and which is not supposed to blow
your brains out, so go easy on those spices.

Shopping:

2 chicken pieces, boned
1 large onion
Garlic
Small piece ginger
Oil
1 bay leaf
2 sticks cinnamon

2 cloves
4 green cardamoms
Salt and pepper
Sugar
3 tablespoons plain yoghurt
1 carton single cream

Cut the chicken into bite-sized pieces. Peel the onion, garlic and ginger, chop roughly, then place in a liquidizer with a splash of cold water. Fry the liquidized onion mixture in hot oil, add all the spices and a sprinkling of sugar. When the mixture starts to brown, add the chicken pieces to the pan. After about 15 minutes the chicken should be sealed and a golden colour, so pour in the yoghurt and leave for a few minutes before finishing it off with the cream. Don't let the sauce come to the boil, as the cream and yoghurt will separate.

ONION BHAJEES

*You can get gram flour from ethnic shops... you think
these bhajees are going to fall apart, but as soon as they
start frying, the egg and the sticky gram flour binds
them together.*

Shopping:

1 onion
Salt
Mild curry powder
Sesame seeds
2 eggs
3 tablespoons gram flour
Oil

Mint sauce:
Plain yoghurt
Sugar
Concentrated mint sauce

Chop the onion into thin slices and put it into a bowl with
the salt, a sprinkling of curry powder and some sesame
seeds. Mix in the eggs, then bind it all together with the
gram flour. Add a little extra flour if the bhajees are not
sticky enough. Next form into patties, heat the oil and
shallow-fry the patties, turning when golden.

Make the mint sauce by simply mixing the yoghurt
with a little mint and a spoonful of sugar.

ENGLISH CURRY

In true Get Stuffed!! style, this recipe uses ultra-cheap cooked meat-ends to create a really delicious meal. The meat-ends are those bits of meat which do not cut properly and which most butchers are too embarrassed to display – sometimes it needs a bit of sorting out with the fingers to get rid of bits of string, gristle or plastic wrapping (especially off salami).

Shopping:

$\frac{3}{4}$ lb meat-ends, cooked
2 onions
$\frac{1}{4}$ lb mushrooms
Oil
1 piece ginger

1 green pepper
$\frac{1}{2}$ pint single cream
2 dessertspoons curry paste
Salt
Rice, cooked

Remove the yucky bits and chop the meat into chunks. Slice the onions and mushrooms and fry in oil. Chop up about 1 inch of ginger and roughly cut up the pepper – add to the frying vegetables. Cook for a few minutes until the vegetables soften, then add the meat chunks, curry paste and cream. Stir in well so the cream doesn't curdle and bring to the boil. Put the lid on the pan and simmer for 10 minutes. Serve with rice.

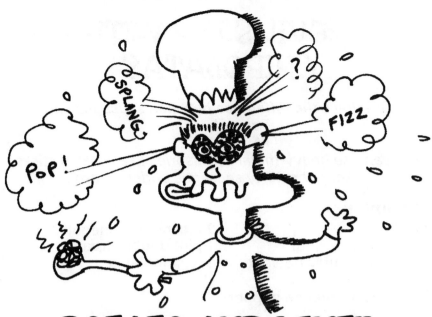

POTATO AND LENTIL CURRY

This is one of those great recipes which you can alter to suit your mood and the scrapings left in the kitchen – have whatever spices you want, and in whatever quantities.

Shopping:

3-4 potatoes
1 onion
Garlic
1 packet red lentils
Oil
Curry paste

Ginger
4 cardamoms, crushed
Black pepper
1 vegetable stock cube
1 lemon

Peel the potatoes and cut into pieces. Chop the onion and garlic and fry with the potatoes. Add the lentils and spices in your preferred quantities together with the stock. Squeeze in the lemon and add the grated lemon rind. Stir and leave to simmer for 20 minutes, adding extra liquid if the mixture begins to dry out.

DEVIL'S DIP WITH CHIPOLATAS

Q: What's the difference between sausages and chipolatas?
A: The SIZE!
You can use heavy-metal accessories like cocktail sticks to keep the party sausages under control.

Shopping:

1 oz butter
3 tablespoons flour
$\frac{1}{2}$ teaspoon curry powder
1 stock cube
$\frac{1}{2}$ teaspoon cayenne pepper

2 teaspoons vinegar
$\frac{1}{4}$ pint double cream
1 lb chipolatas
Oil

ANDY B

BRRRRRM !

Melt the butter in the saucepan and stir in the flour and curry powder, cook for 2–3 minutes. Stir the stock cube into half a pint of boiling water and add to the saucepan gradually, stirring as the spicy roux sauce thickens. Add the cayenne pepper and vinegar. Take the pan off the heat and allow to cool. Whip the cream until stiff and fold it into the cool sauce. Meanwhile, prick the chipolatas, and fry in oil. When they are cooked through, put them on to cocktail sticks and dip into the 'hot' sauce.

CHICKEN CURRY

Why spend hard-earned dosh on Indian take-aways every night when you could cook a fantastic one all by yourself.

Shopping:

1 large chicken fillet
Butter
1 onion
1 red pepper
Curry powder

Flour
1 pint milk
Mango chutney
Rice, cooked

Your butcher will bone your chicken for you or you can do it yourself with a sharp knife. Take off the remaining fat and then chop the fillet into chunks and fry in butter. Chop the onion, de-core and slice the pepper and add to the pan. Sprinkle on the curry powder and flour, as both will soak up the butter and then gradually add the milk on a low heat. The great thing about adding the milk to a pan full of ingredients, is that the sauce doesn't go lumpy. Make sure the chicken is properly cooked through. Add mango chutney to taste and serve with cooked rice.

CHICKEN ENCHILADAS

For gastro-gringos everywhere, enchiladas are a popular Mexican nosh – a bit like pancakes only they're not. They are spicy and cool and they're Mexican! You can buy tortillas (which are the pancakey bit) in any good delicatessen or health shop.

Shopping:

1 chicken leg
1 red pepper
1 green pepper
Mushrooms
Oil
Cheese
Tortillas

Salsa:
1 tin tomatoes
2–3 chillis
Coriander
Cheese

Boil the chicken leg for 30 minutes in lots of water. Chop up the peppers and mushrooms and fry them in a small amount of oil for a few minutes. Shred the chicken into little pieces, being careful to remove all the bone and gristle. Grate the cheese and then lay the mushrooms, peppers, chicken and cheese across the centre of the tortilla in a line. Roll it up and cover with salsa.

Salsa is a very spicy dip made by blending half a tin of tomatoes with chopped chillis and coriander. Spoon the salsa over the tortillas and cover in grated cheese. Put in the oven for 30 minutes at about 180°C (350°F, Gas Mark 4).

CHILLI CON CARNE

It is best to have a tin of red kidney beans handy. If you do cook them from scratch it's important to make sure they're properly soaked before cooking. Ideally soak overnight.

Shopping:

Red kidney beans
1 onion
Garlic
$\frac{1}{2}$ lb minced beef
Oil
1 red pepper
1 green pepper

Mushrooms
1 tin tomatoes
Tomato purée
Salt and pepper
Chilli powder
Rice, cooked

Chop the onion and crush the garlic. Fry the mince, onion and garlic together – you won't need much oil in the pan as the fat in the meat will probably be enough to keep it from sticking. Stir until brown and chop up the other vegetables – mushrooms, green and red peppers and any other eatables at hand. Drain the kidney beans and add to the frying-pan with the tomatoes, tomato purée, salt, pepper and the chilli – as much of this as you want, depending on how much water is at hand. Lower the heat and bubble a bit longer. Serve with rice.

FIRE-DRAGON PIE

So-called because of the fire in the chilli. This is a real winter warmer – how hot can you take it?

Shopping:

3–4 potatoes	1 tin kidney beans
Lentils	Chilli sauce
Oil	Tomato purée
1 onion	Herbs
Garlic	Milk
1 green pepper	Butter

Scrape the potatoes leaving some of the skin on for the fibre and cut into pieces. Boil the potatoes and lentils in separate pans. Heat the oil in a frying-pan. Chop the onion, garlic and pepper and add to the frying-pan. Drain the lentils and the tin of kidney beans ('cause you don't want to eat that nasty, yucky juice) and mix them with all the stuff in the frying-pan. Put into a casserole dish. Add the hot chilli sauce, water, tomato purée and herbs. Mash the potatoes with milk and butter and layer the potato on top of the beany-lentily goo. Cook in the oven for about 25 minutes at 180°C (350°F, Gas Mark 4) until the top is crispy and crunchy.

PIZZA AND PASTA:

When you go to the pub, line your gut with pasta,
It'll soak up the booze and make you 'lasta'.

SPAGHETTI RAGU

*If you are just no good at twiddling all that spaghetti stuff
on to your fork, be seriously clever and break the
spaghetti into little pieces before you boil it and then you
don't even have to cut it when it's on your plate!
To see if your spaghetti is cooked, throw it against the
wall and if it sticks it's ready. This is also a creative and
entirely new concept in wallpaper – remember you
heard it here first, kids!*

Shopping:

Oil	Basil
1 onion	Oregano
Garlic	Salt and pepper
$\frac{1}{2}$ lb minced beef	Spaghetti
1 tin tomatoes	Parmesan

Fry the chopped onion and garlic in a little oil until it's
soft and then add the meat and keep stirring until it's all
brown. Add the tomatoes, herbs, salt and pepper and
simmer gently for about 1 hour, stirring occasionally. If
the mixture looks as if it is drying out, add some water,
stock or red wine. Cook your pasta in boiling, salted
water, drain and pour the sauce over the spaghetti.
Sprinkle grated Parmesan on top.

SPAGHETTI CARBONARA

This is a real quickie Italian meal that's great as a lunch snack. English people like to wallop loads of Parmesan on top, but it tastes better with just a sprinkling of black pepper.

Shopping:

Spaghetti
Salt
Bacon
Oil

2 eggs
Parmesan
Black pepper

Boil a saucepan of salted water and add the spaghetti, curling it around the pan so that it all goes in. Cook for as long as it says on the packet. De-rind the bacon, cut into thin strips and then fry. Drain the pasta and stir in the bacon pieces. Break the eggs into the pasta and bacon, and put back on to the heat, keep stirring for a couple of minutes until the eggs have cooked on to the spaghetti. Sprinkle with whatever takes your fancy.

92

MACARONI CHEESE

Good old British pasta at its best and cheapest and it doesn't have to taste like that slop at school.

Shopping:

Macaroni
Cheese
1 tablespoon cornflour
$\frac{3}{4}$ pint milk

1 teaspoon mustard
Butter/margarine
2 tomatoes
Salt and pepper

Take a saucepan, some water and some salt, put them all together and boil that macaroni – look at the packet to see how long it needs to cook. Grate absolutely loads of cheese. Mix the cornflour and a little milk together and make sure that there are no lumpy bits. Drain the macaroni and leave it in the saucepan on the heat. Pour in the cornflour paste, more milk and the cheese, and stir. Add some mustard and keep stirring until the sauce thickens. Grease an oven dish, spoon in the mixture and sprinkle grated cheese on top with slices of tomato and a touch of pepper. Brown in the oven for 30 minutes at 180°C (350°F, Gas Mark 4).

PASTA IN TUNA SAUCE

The sauce only takes as long as the pasta. How long is that? Well, read the packet, duffer!

Shopping:

Pasta
1 onion
2 sticks celery
Oil

1 tin tuna fish
1 tin tomatoes
Salt and pepper

Put the pasta into hot water and boil. Chop the onion and celery and fry until they go soft. Drain the tuna and add to the pan with the tomatoes, salt, pepper, and cook for 10 minutes. Use fresh tomatoes if you've got some as they will taste better. If it starts to dry out, add a little water. When the pasta is *al dente* (soft!), drain, and mix the tuna sauce into the pasta, sprinkling Parmesan on top.

TUNA BAKE

Always have a tin of tuna handy – if nothing else, you can always eat it straight out of the tin or feed your cat with it!

Shopping:

Pasta
1 onion
2–3 courgettes
Mushrooms
Oil
Garlic
1 tin tomatoes

Tomato purée
Herbs
1 tin tuna fish
1 medium carton cottage
  cheese
Butter/margarine
Cheese

Cook the pasta in boiling water. Meanwhile chop the onion, courgettes and mushrooms. Heat the oil in a frying-pan and add the onion. When they're sizzling nicely, add the courgettes and mushrooms. Crush the garlic and add to the frying-pan together with the tin of tomatoes, tomato purée, herbs and a tin of drained tuna. Drain off the pasta and mix the cottage cheese into the pasta. Layer the pasta and the tomato/tuna stuff in a greased ovenproof dish and sprinkle with grated cheese. Put into the oven for 15–20 minutes at about 180°C (350°F, Gas Mark 4).

PIZZA

This is a good party meal idea if you buy ready-made bases. With all the ingredients laid out and a hot oven handy, your guests can prepare their own pizza and cook it themselves when they're hungry. Be sure to start off with a base of tomato and finish off with a dash of oil – the rest is up to you.

Shopping:

Pizza bases
1 tin tomatoes, chopped
Cheese
1 green pepper
Mushrooms
1 onion

Ham
1 tin tuna fish
1 tin pineapple pieces
Tomatoes
Olive oil
Italian seasoning

If you're brave you can make your own dough for the bases or you can be clever and buy them ready-made. Spoon the tomatoes on to the base, covering with grated cheese. Chop up all the vegetables you are using – pepper, mushrooms, onion – and spread over the top of the pizza base. Add the tuna, ham, pineapple, sliced tomatoes and anything else you can balance on the top. Sprinkle with olive oil (so it doesn't dry out in the oven) and Italian seasoning and slam it in the oven for 10 minutes at 180°C (350°F, Gas Mark 4). For an extra-funky pizza you can add things like pepperoni, capers and anchovies. For some reason pizzas taste better if you're a bit frugal with the topping, rather than over-generous – saves money too!

PASTA SALAD

Cold pasta salad is a good summer snack and what all picnic hampers are made of. It's also an excellent way of using up leftover pasta.

Shopping:

Pasta
1 red pepper
1 green pepper
Oil
Salt

1 tin tuna fish
1 carrot
Garlic powder
Parsley

Cook the pasta in salted water as per the packet instructions. De-seed the peppers and cut into strips. Fry the peppers in hot oil with a pinch of salt. Drain the pasta and run under the cold tap until it's cool. Open the tuna and flake in its own oil. Peel and grate the carrot. Mix everything together and add a little parsley as a garnish.

SCRAPS:

Don't chuck leftover food away,
Cook and scoff another day.

BACON SCRAP PIE

A meal made from those grotty bacon off-cuts that don't look very nice, but are really cheap. They can be a bit salty, so don't add any extra salt along the way.

Shopping:

2 onions
2 carrots
Oil
4 large potatoes

1 packet bacon scraps
Butter
Milk
Black pepper

Chop the onions and grate the carrots. Fry in oil for 5 minutes or so to soften. Spoon into the bottom of a greased casserole dish. Peel the potatoes and boil. De-rind the bacon and cut into bite-sized pieces. Add a bit more oil to the frying-pan and fry the bacon. Layer the cooked bacon on top of the onion and carrot. Drain the potatoes and mash with butter and milk and a little pepper. Spread the potato over the top and pop it in the oven for about 40 minutes at 180°C (350°F, Gas Mark 4).

LEFTOVER CHICKEN SOUP

If you've just woken up after a seriously wild party and the house is wrecked and there's only party scraps left in the kitchen and the cash dispenser won't give you any money, you can make this – yum, yum.

Shopping: (there isn't any!)

Chicken carcass
1 onion
Oil
1 potato

Garlic
Salt and pepper
1 chicken stock cube

Pull the chicken scraps off the carcass, making sure you don't get any little bones. Chop the onion and fry in some oil with the pieces of chicken. Chop the potato – you don't need to bother peeling it if you scrub the skin. Add the potato, salt, pepper and chopped garlic to the saucepan. Pour some boiling water over your stock cube, stirring, then add it to the pan – pour in enough water to cover everything – bring to the boil and simmer for about 25 minutes. The soup should thicken as the stock evaporates and it'll start to taste really good. Put it all into a liquidizer and blend. If you haven't got one you'll just have to eat soup with lumps in it – it's just as tasty.

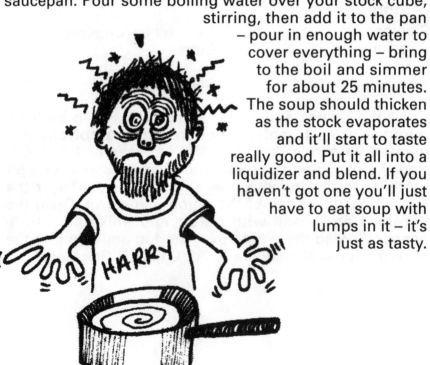

INSALATA DI RISO

If you made too much rice last night and you're not getting married in the morning, one thing you can do is make Insalata di Riso – or rice salad to you 'non-Italianos'.

Shopping:

1 egg	Cheese
Tomatoes	1 tin tuna fish
Carrots	Mayonnaise
Celery	Rice, cooked

Put an egg into cold water and boil for 10 minutes. Wash all your salad vegetables and chop the tomatoes, celery, carrots and cheese into cubes. When the egg is hard-boiled, shell and cut into little pieces and add the whole lot to the leftover rice. Drain the tuna and mix this in as well. Bind it together with mayonnaise and dollop the ricey-gooey salad into a bowl and put in the fridge to cool. Delicious in the summer.

BUBBLE AND SQUEAK

This is a great way to use up all those vegetable leftovers that are sitting in the saucepans from the dinner party you had three weeks ago – but don't use anything with funny growths sprouting out of it. The most exciting thing about this recipe is that you can shape your patties into whatever you want – piggies, sheep or other equally wild and outrageous forms. Yes – it's fun for all the family.

Shopping: (there isn't any!)

Potatoes, cooked and
  mashed
Carrots, cooked
Cabbage, cooked
Cheese

Salt and pepper
Oregano
1 egg
Oil

Simply put all your leftovers into a big saucepan and mash them up together. Shove in some salt and pepper, oregano and handfuls of grated cheese. Bind it together with an egg (or 2 eggs if you have a lot of vegetables to use up) and make into patties with your clean handies. Fry in hot oil and turn to brown on both sides. You could also grill the patties – just brush them with some oil first. Serve with lashings of tomato ketchup.

DON'T BE AFRAID TO GET OUT YOUR KETCHUP!

NOT VERY CLEVER!

RICE WITH ANYTHING

The most marvellous, wonderful, groovy thing about this recipe is ... that, except for the rice, you can ignore the ingredients completely and use anything you've got in your fridge instead!

Shopping:

1 onion
Broccoli
1 green pepper
Few rashers bacon
Oil

1 large tin tomatoes
Salt and pepper
Rice
Cheese
Parsley

Chop up your onion, a few florets of broccoli and the green pepper. De-rind and cut up the bacon. Heat some oil in a frying-pan and add the onion and bacon. When the onion goes soft, add the broccoli and peppers. Cook for a few minutes before adding the tomatoes and seasoning. Measure out 1 cup of rice and pour into the pan with 1 cup of water. You don't need much water as you already have the liquid from the tomatoes. Bring to the boil, turn the heat down and simmer for 20 minutes – add some more boiling water if it starts to dry out. Grate the cheese and chop the parsley. When the rice is cooked, serve and sprinkle the cheese and parsley over the top.

AFTERNOON TEA:

If you crave cakes in the afternoon,
Here's some stuff to make you swoon.

CARROT CAKE

This is so easy to make that your pet rabbit could do it for you, but watch carefully to make sure bunny doesn't hurt his paws when grating that carrot.

Shopping:

4 oz carrot
Raisins
1 dessertspoon rum
1 oz hazelnuts, chopped
5 oz wholemeal flour

$\frac{1}{2}$ teaspoon baking powder
$\frac{1}{2}$ teaspoon allspice
2 oz muscovado sugar
3 eggs

Grate the carrot. Mix together a handful of raisins, the rum and chopped hazlenuts. Sift the flour and mix with the baking powder and allspice. Weigh out the sugar and mix the eggs into it. Dissolve the sugar into the eggs over a pan of hot water so you get a nice paste. Whisk for about 3 minutes. Pour the flour into the sugar and egg and then add the carrot and raisin mixture. Dollop it into a tin and put in the oven for about 30 minutes at 180°C (350°F, Gas Mark 4). Surprise, surprise – it doesn't taste of carrots.

SCONES

*Do you say scone as in bone, or scone as in Babylon.
Well, kids, whether you're posh or not doesn't matter, so
long as you like lashings of cream and jam and more
cream and more cream and more...!*

Shopping:

8 oz flour
$\frac{1}{2}$ teaspoon salt
$1\frac{1}{2}$ oz lard
1 tablespoon sugar
4 dessertspoons sultanas
1 egg

Milk
Butter/margarine
Cream
Jam
Butter

Sieve the flour and salt into a bowl and rub in the lard with your fingertips until the mixture looks like breadcrumbs. Add the sultanas and sugar and stir in with a knife, as this lets more air into the mixture. Beat the egg with a fork and add a little of the egg and some milk to form a soft dough. Roll out the dough on a floured surface, with a floured rolling pin, until it is about 1 inch thick. Cut out rounds of dough with a pastry cutter and place on a greased baking tray. Glaze each scone with the rest of the beaten egg, using a pastry brush, and put into the oven for 12 minutes at 240°C (475°F, Gas Mark 9). Serve with oodles of cream, cream and more cream – well, you can have jam and butter as well if you like!

KAISERSCHMAN

A German recipe involving a lot of floury dough. It is very important to 'ruhren' and 'ruhren' all the way through this, so you don't ruin it!

Shopping:

4 oz flour
$\frac{1}{4}$ pint milk
2 dessertspoons sugar
2 teaspoons baking
   powder

Vanilla flavouring
Raisins
2 eggs
Oil
Icing sugar/jam

Mix the flour, milk, sugar, baking powder and vanilla flavouring together in a whopping bowl and *ruhren* (German for 'stir' in case you hadn't worked that out). Sprinkle in as many raisins as you want and mix. Separate the eggs, adding the yolks to the rest and whisking the whites until they are fluffy – then gently fold them in. Heat the oil in a frying-pan – pour in the mixture and stir it for about 5-10 minutes as it cooks and goes into lumpy bits. Serve with jam or a sprinkling of icing sugar.

BROWNIES

No – not small Girl Guides, they're biscuity chocolatey things. Brownies are a popular American munchie.

Shopping:

3 oz butter/margarine
5 oz light brown sugar
3 oz dark brown sugar
1 tablespoon instant coffee
1 tablespoon hot water

1 egg
6 oz plain flour
1 teaspoon baking powder
6 oz plain chocolate

Melt the butter and sugar in a saucepan over a very gentle heat. Dissolve the coffee in the hot water and stir into the pan. Remove from the heat and allow the dark paste to cool a little before whisking in the egg. Sieve the flour and baking powder and fold into the mixture. Break the chocolate into pea-sized pieces, so it melts more easily, and stir them into the sticky goo. Grease a baking tray and pour in the lumpy brownie mixture – the chocolate pieces will melt in the oven. Cook for 30 minutes at 180°C (350°F, Gas Mark 4). Leave to cool for 10 minutes before cutting into pieces.

CHOCOLATE BISCUIT CAKE

This is a cake you don't even need to bake. It is a slimming meal – the very latest for people on a strict diet of chocolate and sugar.

Shopping:

8 oz digestive biscuits
4 oz butter/margarine
3 oz golden syrup

1 oz cocoa powder
2 oz seedless raisins
4 oz plain cooking chocolate

Grease the cake tin and crush those biscuits. Measure out all the other ingredients except for the cooking chocolate and biscuits and mix them together into a wonderfully stodgy mess. Stir in the biscuits and pour into the tin. Cool in the fridge. Meanwhile melt the chocolate in a bowl over some hot water and pour over the cake. Put back into the fridge and ages later it will be solid and ready to scoff.

CHEESE ANIMALS

Cheese straws are boring, so what you guys want to do is make the dough into cheese animals – elephants, heffalumps, giraffes, dinosaurs, plankton, whatever. Make sure there's an adult present as creative types can get carried away with this dish.

Shopping:

4 oz self raising flour
Pinch of salt
Pinch of paprika

2 oz margarine
3 oz cheese
1 egg

Sift the flour and add the salt, paprika and margarine. Rub in the margarine to form a breadcrumb-like consistency. Grate the cheese and mix in. Beat the egg and add to the bowl to bind it all together into a stiff paste. Roll out the dough on a floured surface and cut into shapes – brilliant, make your friends guess what the shapes are supposed to be! Place on a greased baking tray and cook for 15–20 minutes at 190°C (375°F, Gas Mark 5).

DESSERTS:

If you like eating puds and jelly,
Shove some of this goo in your belly.

PROFITEROLES

If 'profiteroles' didn't sound so poncy more people would eat them.

Shopping:

2 oz butter
$\frac{1}{4}$ pint water
4 oz plain flour
Salt

2 eggs
1 medium bar chocolate
Cream, spray or whipped

Melt the butter on a low heat, add the water and bring to the boil. Sift the flour and pinch of salt and add to the butter and water. Beat the eggs and pour in a little at a time. Grease a baking tray and blob on the choux pastry mix. Put in the oven for 20 minutes at 180°C (350°F, Gas Mark 4). When they are done, the profiteroles will puff up and become hollow inside so you can squeeze in the cream – but allow them to cool before you do this or the cream will melt all over the place. Melt the chocolate in a bowl over some hot water and then pour it over the profiteroles.

Mystery chef announcement:
'Choux pastry is nothing to do with shoes.'

CHOCOLATE MARQUISE

Heaven for chocoholics. You can get very good quality cooking chocolate from a delicatessen – it works out much cheaper than buying sweet shop stuff.

Shopping:

1 lb dark chocolate
8 oz butter

4 eggs
6 oz icing sugar

Break the chocolate into pieces and put in a bowl over a pan of hot water to melt. Cut the butter up, so it will melt more quickly, and add to the chocolate. Meanwhile, separate the eggs and whisk the icing sugar into the egg yolks until the mixture goes pale. You use icing sugar for this because it's finer than ordinary sugar and won't leave lumps. Beat the egg whites in a separate bowl until they go fluffy and form peaks. Add the melted chocolatey-butter liquid to the sugary egg yolks and mix, then carefully fold the whisked egg whites into the chocolate mixture. Pour into bowls, moulds, whatever you've got lying around, and pop into the fridge to set. If the mould is cool it will help the chocolate to set more quickly – if you line the mould with clingfilm, it'll be easier to get the Marquise out. Hours later you can eat it.

LES CRÊPES

This means pancakes in French and these are flambéed in Grand Marnier – oh la la!

Shopping:

9 oz flour
2 eggs
$\frac{1}{4}$ pint milk

Oil
Sugar
Grand Marnier

Mix the flour, eggs and milk together in a liquidizer until they form a smooth liquid. You can do this by hand if you don't have a liquidizer. Heat a touch of oil in a frying-pan and pour in a little of the *crêpe* mixture, so it just covers the bottom of the pan. Cook on one side and then flip expertly on to the other side. Sprinkle sugar on the *crêpe* and then pour on a glug of Grand Marnier and set light to it with a match. Don't eat it until the flames have gone out, kids!

TRIFLE

A great excuse to use up all those daft things that have been sitting in the back of the cupboard – like hundreds and thousands, jelly diamonds and all those other things you had on your birthday cake when you were six. You can use any fruit and any flavour of jelly – the possibilities are endless.

Shopping:

1 packet sponge fingers
Sherry
1 tin of fruit
1 packet jelly
2 tablespoons custard
   powder

1 tablespoon sugar
1 pint milk
Spray cream
Decorations

Break up the sponge fingers and put them at the bottom of a bowl. Sprinkle sherry over the sponge and then pour over the fruit and some of the juice from the tin. Make the jelly following the instructions on the packet and pour over the fruit. Put the bowl into the fridge for the jelly to set and then make the custard. Mix the custard powder and sugar with a little milk to make a paste, then add hot milk and put on to heat until it thickens. Leave the custard to cool, then pour it on top of the trifle and put in the fridge – AGAIN! Ages later it has set and you can cover with spray cream, Flake, hundreds and thousands, jelly diamonds, almond flakes – very pretty. The sherry at the bottom ensures that home-made trifle is always appreciated!

RICE PUDDING

Most rice has the instructions for rice pud written on the packet – so read it, dummies! This is definitely one of those dishes which has been ruined by its association with school dinner – but it's very tasty if you do it properly. It's also excellent for lining your stomach before an alcoholic binge. If you serve it at a dinner party, you can initiate weird conversations to find out if your guests like rice pudding skins, or not.

Shopping:

1 packet pudding rice
Butter
1 pint milk

1 dessertspoon sugar
Cinnamon

You need twice as much water as rice, so boil 2 cups of rice in 4 cups of water until the rice swells and soaks up all the water. Grease an ovenproof dish with butter. Drain the rice when it's ready and de-starch by putting it in a sieve and pouring boiling water through. Pour it into the bowl and cover with milk. Add sugar and a knob of butter to make it creamier. Pop it into the oven for as long as it says on the packet, at about 200°C (400°F, Gas Mark 6). Eat with dollops of jam.

Do YOU LIKE THE SKIN?

APPLE PIE

If you want to mother someone, cook them this. If you want to cheat, use ready-made pastry. Don't forget to buy cooking apples.

Shopping:

Filling:
1½ lb Bramley apples
1 oz brown sugar
¼ teaspoon ground cloves
3 oz raisins
2 tablespoons water
Pinch of grated nutmeg

Pastry:
4 oz plain flour
4 oz self raising flour
4 oz margarine
Pinch of salt
Cold water

Peel the apples, cut into quarters and take out the core. Slice them thinly and put in a saucepan with the sugar, spice and raisins. Sprinkle with water and cook on a low heat for 10 minutes. Leave to cool.

Meanwhile rub the flour, salt and margarine together until it forms a breadcrumb-like consistency. Add some water and gather it together into a ball. Roll out half the pastry on a floured surface and press into the bottom of a greased pie dish. Fill with the apple mixture. Roll out the rest of the pastry and lay over the top of the apple, pressing it down around the edges. Cut a cross in the centre of the pie to let the steam out while it's cooking. Bake in the oven for 30 minutes at 200°C (400°F, Gas Mark 6).

FRUITY TOFU GOO

Silken tofu is a bit like yoghurt, but rather flavourless...
it is often used to form the basis of tofu desserts and is a
dairy-free alternative for vegans and vegetarians.
Shelling all these nuts will really get you going.

Shopping:

2 oz pistachio nuts	4 tablespoons honey
8 oz silken tofu	1 tin pear halves

Shell the pistachio nuts and chop into little pieces. Blend the tofu in a liquidizer until it's creamy, then add the honey and blend this in. If you haven't got a liquidizer your tofu will be lumpy and won't taste as good – tough luck! Drain the juice from the pears and pour the tofu sauce over the pears, sprinkling on the nuts for that crunchy topping. Chill in the fridge for about 30 minutes and scoff.

RHUBARB CRUMBLE

A Sunday lunch time filler –
'The gang will all start bopping
when they taste that sexy topping.'

Shopping:

2 lb rhubarb
Sugar
Cinnamon
Lemon juice

Topping:
4-6 oz plain flour
Handful of porridge oats
Brown sugar
3 oz butter
Muscovado sugar
Chopped almonds

Wash the rhubarb and chop into 1 inch pieces. Cook the rhubarb in a saucepan with 1 cup of water, a sprinkling of sugar, cinnamon and a good shot of lemon juice. Let it simmer away, but do not cook for more than about 10–15 minutes as it will go mushy.

Rhubarb →

← more Rhubarb

For the crumble, mix the flour, sugar and oats in a bowl and rub in the butter until the mixture goes crumbly. Add more butter or flour to get the right consistency. Pour the stewed rhubarb into an ovenproof dish and cover with oodles of the sexy topping. For extra decoration, sprinkle chopped almonds and muscovado sugar on the top. Cook in the oven for 25 minutes at about 190°C (375°F, Gas Mark 5), until it is brown on top.

CARAMELISED APPLES

The sauce is a bit complicated, but you could always use spray cream instead. It's an excellent way to turn healthy, green things into unhealthy, golden things.

Shopping:

4 apples	*Sauce:*
Butter	1 egg yolk
Brown sugar	White wine
White wine	Brown sugar

Peel the apples, halve them and remove the core. Slice the apples thinly and arrange into a fan shape. Melt some butter in a frying-pan, slide in the apples and cover with a good sprinkling of brown sugar. Spoon the melted butter over the apples as they cook. When the apples are becoming tender, pour in about a quarter of the bottle of white wine, spoon over the apples and then bring to the boil. Next, put the frying-pan under a grill until the apples begin to brown.

To make the fluffy sauce, separate the egg and whisk the yolk, a little white wine and a pinch of brown sugar over a very gentle heat until the yolk mixture goes light and fluffy. Don't leave on the heat for too long or it will burn. Pour the sauce on a plate and place the apples on top – highly artistic!

PEARS ON FRENCH BREAD

A brilliantly easy dessert. Just whop on that cholesterol with piles of butter and excessive amounts of sugar – yes, it's serious heartburn time.

Shopping:

1 stick French bread, stale   2 lb pears
1 packet unsalted butter   Brown sugar

Slice the bread, and butter on both sides – no skimping on the butter! Peel and de-core the pears before slicing them into wafer-thin pieces. Lay the pear halves on top of the bread and smother with brown sugar. Whack into the oven for 20 minutes at about 160°C (325°F, Gas Mark 3). Serve it on its own or with cream.

GERMAN BANANAS

This is a buttery, almondy, bananary dessert with a totally crazy sauce!

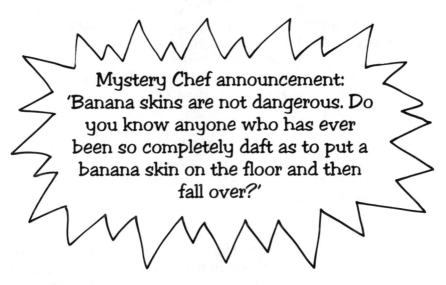

Mystery Chef announcement: 'Banana skins are not dangerous. Do you know anyone who has ever been so completely daft as to put a banana skin on the floor and then fall over?'

Shopping:

2 bananas
Butter
Oil
Almonds
1 dessertspoon honey

Sauce:
1 carton fromage frais/sour cream
White German wine
Cornflour

Peel the bananas and slice them lengthwise into 2 halves. Melt the butter in the pan and add a little oil so the butter doesn't burn, then fry the bananas lightly. Sprinkle with almonds and honey. Turn the bananas and then take them out of the pan to make the sauce.

Pour the fromage frais over the almonds in the pan and add a little more butter. Dash in some white wine and if the sauce is a bit thin, stir in a little cornflour or thickener. Pour over the bananas.

F.T.C. GINGERBREAD COOKIES

A recipe submitted by Feed The Children, who will even supply special cookie cutters so you can make these cookies! – All the proceeds go to the charity. Contact Feed The Children at 1 Priory Avenue, Caversham, Reading, Berkshire, RG4 7SE.

Shopping:

4 oz butter
4 oz sugar
9 oz plain flour
$\frac{1}{2}$ teaspoon bicarbonate soda

1–2 teaspoons ground ginger
Syrup, warmed

Mix the butter and sugar together until soft and smooth. Work in the flour, soda and ginger and form into a dough by mixing in the warmed syrup. Knead the dough, then roll out on a floured surface. Cut out shapes – whatever takes your fancy – and place them on a greased baking tray. Bake at 180°C (350°F, Gas Mark 4) for 10–15 minutes. Allow to cool slightly before lifting on to a wire rack. The mixture makes about 20–30 cookies.

INDEX

potato and lentil curry,
85
TVP curry, 74

D
devil's dip with
chipolatas, 86

E
easy chicken casserole,
60
eggs:
bacon and egg bake, 19
basic quiche, 24
cheesy pie, 25
egg and lentil bake, 23
egg and salami surprise,
22
eggy toasties, 7
fish flan, 35
mushroom omelette, 21
Persian scrambled eggs,
20
English curry, 84
English rarebit, 10
enchiladas, chicken, 88

F
fire-dragon pie, 90
fish:
blackened fish, 30
cheesy fish grill, 27
fish flan, 35
fish in a parcel, 34
fish in breadcrumbs, 29
fish stew, 31
insalata di riso, 103
mackerel in garlic and
olive oil, 33
moules marinière, 36
pasta in tuna sauce, 94
pasta salad, 99

poached fish, 32
prawn provençale, 38
slashed fish with yoghurt
and spices, 28
stuffed sprats, 37
tuna bake, 96
fruity tofu goo, 119
F.T.C. gingerbread cookies,
124

G
gingerbread cookies,
F.T.C., 124
German bananas, 123
Greek salad, 80
green pie, 72

H
ham:
ham and mushroom
crumble, 48
ham and leeks, 49
honeyed pork chops, 45
hummus, 12

I
insalata di riso,103

K
kaiserschman, 109
kartoffelkloss mit
specksoss, 16
kartoffel puffer, 15
konbu no nimono, 78
kidneys:
lambs' kidneys, 66
steak and kidney
pudding, 41

L
lamb:
lamb medallions, 54